# COZY VEGAN
# PIES AND TARTS

## 60 Plant-Based Recipes That Taste Like Home

HELEN AU, Creator of With Helen

PAGE STREET
PUBLISHING CO.

First published in 2022 by
Page Street Publishing Co.
27 Congress Street, Suite 1511
Salem, MA  01970
www.pagestreetpublishing.com

Distributed by Macmillan, sales in Canada by The Canadian Manda Group.

26    25    24    23    22     1   2    3    4    5

ISBN-13: 978-1-64567-655-3
ISBN-10: 1-64567-655-2

Library of Congress Control Number: 2022934678

Cover and book design by Kylie Alexander for Page Street Publishing Co.
Photography by Helen Au

Printed and bound in the United States of America

# DEDICATION

To my younger self, you are worthy the moment you were born.
Everything you dream of can come true.

# INTRODUCTION

As soon as I learned to walk, I followed my mom into the kitchen to watch her cook. I would stand there on my pink plastic stool until I was tall enough to watch without it. My mom had learned all her cooking from my grandmother. She was the only daughter who truly enjoyed cooking, and to this day, she cooks the flavors of my grandmother's home. I love learning where dishes come from and especially how ingredients are used in different cultures. The feeling of flour on my hands . . . of kneading dough . . . of waiting for the ingredients to come together and rise . . . I don't have the words.

I came from a family of chefs, with grandparents from Vietnam who owned restaurants. It is not a surprise that my dad is also a chef. I would say that even though she did not work as a chef, my mom's cooking and baking skills are way better than my dad's. And that's one of the reasons why I risked getting yelled at for bothering her while she cooked or baked. The five-year-old Helen just wanted to start helping her mom in the kitchen and be able to prepare delicious meals for everyone. There is nothing more satisfying than seeing someone you care for enjoying a bite of a warm cookie or slice of pie you just baked and telling you how delicious it is.

Even though I love cooking and baking with my whole heart, there was a period in my life when I didn't have a good relationship with food. In middle school, I started comparing myself to all the girls in my class and on social media. I wanted to fit in and be just like them. As a result, I started to gradually cut out foods that were considered "bad" for me by society—even foods my mom prepared. By the time I was fourteen years old, a sophomore in high school, I had developed anorexia. During that challenging time, my relationship with my parents, especially my mom, deteriorated as we often got into fights and no longer had the connection over food that bonded us before.

It was one of the lowest times of my life, and everything felt like it was falling apart. It wasn't until I was sitting in the emergency room with my father and sister on either side of me, with the doctors begging me to stay in the hospital and receive help, that everything changed. I still remember seeing my dad cry for the first time and hearing the fear in my mom's voice over the phone when I told her I would remain in the hospital to recover. At that moment, I promised myself that I would do nothing that did not bring me happiness. Life is too short and there is too much in this life of ours to celebrate. Most importantly, I learned to love myself fully for who I am.

I wouldn't normally write about this time in my life in a book that celebrates the love of baking, but I do want to let you know how it relates to pies and tarts.

During my recovery journey at the hospital, my mom was not allowed to bring me homemade food, per hospital policy. And because the hospital wasn't close to my home, I only saw my parents once or twice a week. So oftentimes, I was alone.

Most of the hospital food was foreign to me. However, one night, after finishing dinner, I found myself looking forward to dessert. I opened the cover of the dessert plate and was surprised to see that it was a slice of blueberry pie. I couldn't even remember the last time I had eaten a piece of pie, as it was one of the many foods I didn't allow myself to have. I took a small bite and fell in love with it. It was not overly sweet, and (maybe because it was a pie), it felt a little bit like home. I finished the whole slice and felt joy in eating dessert for the first time in a very, very long time.

Since that moment, all forms of pies, especially blueberry, hold a special place in my heart, and I will never forget the feeling that slice of pie brought to my soul. It felt like someone bringing a piece of their home to me. I want to do the same for you—making you feel at home here no matter where you are in this world. I don't want anyone to feel alone and unworthy of love like I did at that time. You being here is a gift to the world.

*   *   *

I became vegan just over two years ago, long after I had recovered and after watching many videos and documentaries about how poorly animals are treated. I never turned back. During this time, I learned that being vegan is not just about the animals and the environment for me, but also a way of looking at life and treating Mother Earth with love and care. It is about learning to love life and everything nature has to offer and to nurture our body and soul the best way we can. It is about living life with intention, and appreciating and loving all the small moments we have every day, whether you are alone or with people you care about.

At the end of the day, being vegan is only a label. What is most important is eating and doing whatever it is that is best for you and makes you light up. You do not need to label yourself vegan to enjoy a slice of delicious, fudgy and melt-in-your-mouth Dreamy Brownie Pie (page 28), Vegan Peanut Butter Cup Tart (page 36) or Unbelievably Creamy Nutella® Pie (page 48). If you just want all the nostalgic, childhood, comforting flavors, head right over to Chapter 2 (page 27) . . . you might have guessed by now that this is my favorite chapter!

Whatever your soul is calling for in this cookbook, enjoy it fully and happily. Everyone is welcome here, and I also included gluten-free crusts options too, in case you or your loved ones adhere to a gluten-free diet.

Every single one of the recipes in this cookbook is made with love, from my tiny kitchen to yours. I am not a professional baker, and you do not need to be one either in order to make a heartwarming pie or tart for you, your family and friends to enjoy. Have lots of fun with these recipes, and know that I will be thinking of you. From my kitchen to yours, please enjoy these vegan pie and tart recipes.

With all my love,

# VEGAN PIE AND TART CRUSTS

One of the reasons I was reluctant to go vegan at first was because of sweets. I couldn't possibly imagine how I could make pastries and buttery, flaky crusts without the use of eggs and other dairy products. However, I was completely wrong. There are so many plant-based products nowadays that not only make creating vegan pastries easy, but also taste the same or (dare I say it) even better than the original, non-vegan version.

This chapter introduces several vegan pie and tart crust recipes that are not difficult to make. I've included gluten-free and non-baked crust options as well. To avoid recipe fails, read over all the ingredients and instructions for the recipe you are interested in making prior to baking. And even though I list specific crust recipes to use for recipes in the other chapters in this book, feel free to substitute them for any of these crusts! Most of the pie recipes only require one batch of the vegan pie crust, but if you want a double or lattice crust, simply double the recipe and be as creative as you want with the top crust. The majority of the crusts here are perfect for both sweet and savory pies and tarts! So, let's have some fun in the kitchen!

# CLASSIC VEGAN PIE CRUST

### Yield: 1 pie crust

This is absolutely one of the best pie crust recipes ever! It is entirely eggless and dairy-free and made with a food processor. Even so, the crust is so flaky and buttery, wowing all eaters whether they are vegan or not. I love using this crust for the Pumpkin Caramel Pie (page 47), the Vegan Peanut Butter and Jelly Hand Pies (page 52) and the Classic Boba Tea Tartlets (page 62)!

### For the Dough

115 g (½ cup) unsalted vegan butter, cut into 1" (2.5-cm) cubes, cold, plus more for greasing pan

220 g (1¾ cups) all-purpose flour, plus more for dusting

50 g (½ cup) powdered sugar

½ tsp fine sea salt

5–10 ml (1–2 tsp) vegan evaporated milk, cold

### For the Glaze

10 g (½ tbsp) maple syrup

28 g (2 tbsp) unsalted vegan butter, melted

Preheat the oven to 350°F (180°C). Grease a 9-inch (23-cm) pie pan with vegan butter or coconut oil, and lightly flour a sheet of parchment paper.

To make the dough, combine the flour, powdered sugar and salt in a food processor and pulse to blend. Scatter the butter cubes over the flour and pulse until the butter is well incorporated. This should only take a few seconds. Add the evaporated milk 1 teaspoon at a time and pulse with each addition. Stop adding the milk when you see soft, moist clumps. The dough is ready when you pinch some dough and it holds together. Shape the dough into a disk. If the dough is still cold, you can roll the dough out. If not, wrap it in plastic wrap or transfer it into an airtight container, and refrigerate for 30 minutes.

Take the dough out of the refrigerator and place it on the center of the floured parchment paper. Lightly flour the dough and cover it with a second sheet of parchment paper. Roll the dough into a round shape that's 12 inches (30 cm) in diameter. Carefully transfer the dough into the pie pan, making sure there is some dough hanging over the top. Trim off the excess dough until you have a ½-inch (1-cm) overhang. Fold the overhanging dough under itself and pinch the crust to make a decorative edge. Using a fork, prick the bottom of the crust in several places. Transfer the crust to the freezer for 5 minutes.

To make the glaze, add the maple syrup and vegan butter to a small bowl, and mix well. Set aside.

To par-bake the crust (also known as blind-baking, meaning to partially bake the pie crust before adding the filling and baking it again), take the crust out of the freezer and brush it with the maple butter glaze. Place a sheet of parchment paper in the middle of the pie crust and add pie weights or dried beans. Bake the crust for 13 to 15 minutes, or until lightly golden. Remove the crust from the oven and let it cool completely before adding the filling.

# GLUTEN-FREE PIE CRUST

Yield: 1 pie crust

Craving a pie but not sure how to make it gluten-free? This is the perfect recipe for you! This crust tastes just like a classic pie crust: rustic, buttery and absolutely irresistible! Since we are using gluten-free flour, the crust can be a little crumbly at the beginning, but work slowly when rolling the dough and make sure your dough is not too dry, and things will come together nicely.

## For the Dough

172 g (¾ cup) unsalted vegan butter, cut into 1" (2.5-cm) cubes, cold, plus more for greasing pan

100 g (¾ cup + 1 tbsp) buckwheat flour, plus more for dusting

90 g (½ cup + 1 tbsp) white rice flour

13 g (1 tbsp) cane sugar

½ tsp fine sea salt

8–15 ml (½–1 tbsp) ice water, plus more if needed

## For the Glaze

10 g (½ tbsp) maple syrup

28 g (2 tbsp) unsalted vegan butter, melted

Preheat the oven to 350°F (180°C). Grease a 9-inch (23-cm) pie pan with vegan butter or coconut oil, and lightly flour a sheet of parchment paper.

To make the dough, combine the buckwheat flour, white rice flour, sugar and salt in a food processor, and pulse to blend. Scatter the butter cubes over the flour and pulse until the butter is well incorporated. This should only take a few seconds. Add the ice water ½ tablespoon (8 ml) at a time and pulse with each addition. Stop adding water when you see soft, moist clumps. The dough is ready when you pinch some dough and it holds together. Shape the dough into a disk. If the dough is still cold, you can roll it out. If not, wrap it in plastic wrap or transfer it into an airtight container and refrigerate for 30 minutes.

Take the dough out of the refrigerator and place it on the center of the floured parchment paper. Lightly flour the dough and cover it with a second sheet of parchment paper. Roll the dough into a round shape that's 12 inches (30 cm) in diameter. Carefully transfer the dough into the pie pan, making sure there is some dough hanging over the top. Trim off the excess dough until you have a ½-inch (1-cm) overhang. Fold the overhang dough under itself and pinch the crust to make a decorative edge. Using a fork, prick the bottom of the crust in several places. Transfer the crust to the freezer for 5 minutes.

To make the glaze, add the maple syrup and vegan butter to a small bowl, and mix well. Set aside.

To par-bake the crust (also known as blind-baking, meaning to partially bake the pie crust before adding the filling and baking it again), take the crust out of the freezer and brush it with the maple butter glaze. Place a sheet of parchment paper in the middle of the pie crust and add pie weights or dried beans. Bake the crust for 13 to 15 minutes, or until it is lightly golden. Remove the crust from the oven and let it cool completely before adding the filling.

# BUTTERY VEGAN GALETTE CRUST

## Yield: 1 galette crust

250 g (2 cups) all-purpose flour, plus more for dusting

30 g (3 tbsp) coconut sugar

¼ tsp fine sea salt

1 tsp apple cider vinegar

145 g (½ cup + 2 tbsp) unsalted vegan butter, cut into 1" (2.5-cm) cubes, cold

45–75 ml (3–5 tbsp) ice water, plus more as needed

If you know me, you know I absolutely love galettes. Galettes are simply a rustic, free-form version of a pie but a bit easier to make. When baked, galette crusts become a beautiful color, and are so flaky and buttery. (For sweet galettes, you can add a hint of sweetness with coarse sugar on top!) This crust is good for both sweet and savory pies and tarts!

Place the flour, coconut sugar and salt in a food processor, and pulse to blend. Add the apple cider vinegar. Scatter the cubed butter over the flour and pulse until the butter is well incorporated.

Add the ice water ½ tablespoon (7 ml) at a time and pulse with each addition. Stop adding water when you see soft, moist clumps. The dough is ready when you pinch some dough and it holds together.

Gather the dough into a ball and flatten it into the shape of a disk. If the dough is still cold, you can roll out the dough and bake the galette according to the instructions of the recipe you are using. If not, wrap it in plastic wrap or transfer it into an airtight container and refrigerate for 30 minutes.

You can also keep the wrapped dough in the refrigerator for up to 2 days or in the freezer for up to 2 months. When you are ready to use the frozen dough, set the dough on the counter at room temperature to soften for 10 to 15 minutes if your home is warm or place it in the refrigerator to defrost overnight.

# VEGAN GRAHAM CRUST

### Yield: 1 crust

155 g (15 full cracker sheets) vegan graham crackers (use a gluten-free variety if needed)

60 g (¼ cup) unsalted vegan butter, melted

You'll never buy a graham pie crust from a grocery store again with this easy and delicious homemade vegan graham crust! It requires only two ingredients and can be baked or left unbaked. Plus, you can easily make this gluten-free.

Place the graham crackers in a food processor and pulse until you start seeing fine crumbs. Pour the crumbs into a bowl. Add the melted vegan butter and mix to combine.

Transfer the crumbs to a 9-inch (23-cm) pie or tart pan, pressing down on all sides until the pan is covered with the crumbs. Finish the pie or tart according to the instructions in the recipe you've chosen.

# VEGAN COOKIES AND CREAM CRUST

Yield: 1 crust

162 g (about 12 cookies) vegan cookies and cream cookies (use gluten-free if needed)

60 g (¼ cup) unsalted vegan butter, melted

If you are a fan of Oreos or any other cookies and cream desserts, this crust is perfect for you! It is made with only two ingredients, and you can either bake it or leave it unbaked. It is one of the easiest homemade crusts ever!

Place the cookies in a food processor and pulse until you start seeing fine crumbs. Pour the crumbs into a bowl. Add the melted vegan butter and mix to combine.

Transfer the crumbs to a 9-inch (23-cm) pie or tart pan, pressing on all sides until the pan is covered with the crumbs. Finish the pie or tart according to the instructions in the recipe you've chosen.

# VEGAN PASTRY TART CRUST

Yield: 1 tart crust

160 g (1 cup) 1 to 1 gluten-free flour (such as Bob's Red Mill® Gluten-Free 1 to 1 Baking Flour)

14 g (2 tbsp) superfine almond flour

75 g (¾ cup) powdered sugar

45 g (⅓ cup) arrowroot powder

¼ tsp fine sea salt

90 g (6 tbsp) unsalted vegan butter, melted

15–30 ml (1–2 tbsp) unsweetened plant-based milk of choice

½ tsp pure vanilla extract

If I only had room for one tart crust in my life, this one would be it. Like all the other pie and tart crust recipes, this one is made quickly in a food processor. It is buttery, not too sweet and flaky without crumbling apart.

Preheat the oven to 375°F (190°C).

Add the gluten-free flour, almond flour, powdered sugar, arrowroot powder and salt to a bowl. Mix until they are well combined.

In a separate bowl, add the melted vegan butter, 1 tablespoon (15 ml) of the plant-based milk and vanilla extract, and mix until they are well combined. Slowly add the flour mixture and mix until a dough forms. The dough will be slightly crumbly, but if you find that the dough is too dry, add the remaining 1 tablespoon (15 ml) of plant-based milk.

Transfer the dough to a 9-inch (23-cm) tart pan, pressing on all the sides until the pan is covered with the crust. Bake the crust for 10 to 12 minutes, or until it is lightly golden. Remove the crust from the oven and let it cool completely before adding your chosen filling.

# VEGAN OAT TART CRUST

Yield: 1 tart crust

10 g (2 tbsp) ground flaxseeds

90 ml (6 tbsp) water

150 g (1⅔ cups) gluten-free oat flour

50 g (½ cup) superfine almond flour

¼ tsp fine sea salt

30 g (2 tbsp) unrefined coconut oil, melted

43 ml (2 tbsp) maple syrup

If you love oats, you're going to love this vegan oat tart crust! It is one of my favorites when I am looking to make a gluten-free tart crust with a rustic flavor. This recipe requires very simple ingredients, and you do not have to roll out the dough at all!

Preheat the oven to 350°F (180°C).

Add the flaxseeds and water to a bowl, and stir until they are well combined. Set the bowl aside for 3 to 5 minutes.

In a separate bowl, add the oat flour, almond flour and salt. Mix until they are well combined.

Add the melted coconut oil and maple syrup to the bowl with the ground flaxseeds, and mix until they are well combined. Slowly add the flour mixture and mix until a dough forms. The dough will be slightly sticky. Transfer the dough to a 9-inch (23-cm) tart pan, pressing on all the sides until the pan is covered with the crust. Bake the crust for 15 minutes. Remove the crust from the oven and let it cool completely before adding your chosen filling.

# NO-BAKE MEDJOOL DATE TART CRUST

Yield: 1 tart crust

50 g (¼ cup) pitted Medjool dates

45 g (½ cup) gluten-free oat flour

21 g (3 tbsp) superfine almond flour

⅛ tsp fine sea salt

15 g (1 tbsp) unrefined coconut oil, melted

I love snacking on Medjool dates, but I also love baking with them! They have the perfect natural sweetness to them and are good in both sweet and savory recipes. So, when I was looking for a no-bake tart crust recipe, dates were a must-have ingredient. This crust is not only vegan, but also gluten-free and refined sugar-free . . . and it requires no baking at all!

Soak the Medjool dates in hot water for at least 1 hour or in warm water overnight. The Medjool dates are ready to be used when they become soft and slightly mushy.

Add the oat flour, almond flour and salt to a food processor, and pulse until the flour is well combined. Add the dates and coconut oil. Blend until a dough forms. The dough will be sticky to the touch.

Transfer the dough to a 9-inch (23-cm) tart pan, pressing on the sides until the dough covers the pan. Place the crust back in the refrigerator until your chosen filling is ready.

# COMFORTING CHILDHOOD FAVORITES

This is easily my favorite chapter in this cookbook! It is loaded with all the classic comfort flavors that many of us grew up with. Think about all the warm, cozy, rich and satisfying sweets that we could never have enough of and would race to the kitchen to get the first bite once they were ready.

All the flavors in this chapter reflect back to those times when I was craving something comforting and wanted to make a delicious sweet for my family. I grew up in Boston, and if you have never been there before, autumn and winter can get cold quickly. After a snowstorm or during winter break from school, I was almost always in the kitchen, baking away and making something that would warm my soul.

I have always had a sweet tooth and could never get enough of desserts, especially anything with chocolate in it (which is one of the reasons why I love this chapter so much). It is filled with chocolate recipes like Dreamy Brownie Pie (page 28), Vegan Snickers® Tart (page 35) and Vegan German Chocolate Tart (page 55). Don't worry though, if you somehow have a non-chocolate lover in your life—there are other fun flavors in this chapter such as Orange Creamsicle Tartlets (page 31) and Peanut Butter and Jelly Hand Pies (page 52).

# DREAMY BROWNIE PIE

## Yield: 1 (9" [23-cm]) pie

### For the Crust
156 g (1¼ cups) all-purpose flour

25 g (¼ cup) cacao powder

50 g (½ cup) powdered sugar

100 g (7 tbsp) unrefined coconut oil, melted

### For the Filling
167 g (1⅓ cups) all-purpose flour

25 g (¼ cup) cacao powder

100 g (½ cup) cane sugar

1 tsp espresso powder

⅛ tsp fine sea salt

188 ml (¾ cup) unsweetened plant-based milk of choice, room temperature

60 ml (¼ cup) coconut cream

80 g (⅓ cup) unrefined coconut oil, melted

1 tsp pure vanilla extract

85 g (½ cup) chopped vegan chocolate (or chocolate chips)

### For the Topping (optional)
Melted vegan chocolate

Have you ever thought it impossible to make a vegan brownie that tastes just like the classic, fudgy version? If so, you'll most definitely change your mind after making this recipe. It is one of the fudgiest and richest brownies you will ever taste, but in the form of a pie. This will make all non-vegans speechless after one bite!

---

Preheat the oven to 350°F (180°C).

To make the crust, add the flour, cacao powder and powdered sugar to a bowl. Mix until they are well combined. Add the melted coconut oil and mix until a dough forms.

Transfer the dough to a 9-inch (23-cm) pie pan, pressing on all the sides until the pan is covered with the dough. Par-bake for 10 minutes. Remove the crust from the oven and let it cool completely before adding the filling. Do not turn off the oven.

While the crust is cooling, make the filling. Add the flour, cacao powder, cane sugar, espresso powder and salt to a bowl, and mix until all the ingredients are combined. In a separate bowl, add the plant-based milk, coconut cream, coconut oil and vanilla extract. Mix until all the ingredients are incorporated. Slowly pour the wet ingredients into the dry ingredients and mix until everything is combined, being careful not to overmix. Fold in the vegan chocolate. Pour the batter into the cooled pie crust. Bake for 20 minutes, or until an inserted toothpick comes out clean. Allow the pie to cool completely before slicing it. Drizzle the pie with the melted vegan chocolate, if using, before serving.

# ORANGE CREAMSICLE TARTLETS

### Yield: 6 (3" [8-cm]) tartlets

### For the Crust
1 Vegan Pastry Tart Crust (page 21), unbaked

### For the Filling
227 g (8 oz) vegan cream cheese, room temperature

75 g (¾ cup) powdered sugar

96 g (1 cup) vegan whipped cream

½ tsp orange zest

1 tsp orange extract

30 ml (2 tbsp) fresh orange juice

1 drop vegan orange food coloring

### For the Topping (optional)
Thinly sliced oranges

Chopped pistachios

Vegan whipped cream

Fresh thyme leaves

I find it hard to believe that there can be non-chocolate lovers in the world, but I do have one in my family (my sister) who does not like chocolate at all. I mean all chocolate flavors. Can you relate? Growing up, whenever my mom bought ice cream for my siblings and me, she would always get one non-chocolate flavor, oftentimes, orange creamsicle. It was not my go-to flavor, but whenever it was too hot out or when I craved something light and refreshing, I would go for orange creamsicle popsicles or ice cream. So, when it came time for me to write this chapter, I knew I had to make a recipe for this flavor. This tart is not only creamy but tastes identical to the classic flavor and is not artificial at all. Prepare to wow your non-chocolate lovers with this recipe!

---

Preheat the oven to 375°F (190°C).

Make the Vegan Pastry Tart Crust. Transfer the dough to six (3-inch [8-cm]) tart pans, pressing on all sides until the pans are covered with the dough. Bake the crusts for 8 to 10 minutes, or until lightly golden. Remove the crusts from the oven and let them cool completely before adding the filling.

For the filling, add the vegan cream cheese and powdered sugar to a bowl. With a hand mixer or stand mixer, whip until combined. Add the vegan whipped cream, orange zest, orange extract, orange juice and 1 drop of orange food coloring. Lightly mix, scraping down the sides of the bowl as needed. If you want the tartlet filling to be more orange, add more food coloring.

Divide the filling into the tart pans. Transfer the tarts to the refrigerator, and let them set for 3 to 4 hours or overnight before serving. Garnish the tarts with some sliced oranges, chopped pistachios, vegan whipped cream and fresh thyme, if using.

# CONFETTI CHEESECAKE TART

## Yield: 1 (9" [23-cm]) tart

Who doesn't like sprinkles? This vegan cheesecake tart is not only easy to make and super creamy, but the sprinkles in the filling give you bursts of rainbow with each bite. This tart has all the same flavors as the confetti birthday cakes you ate growing up.

### For the Crust
1 Vegan Graham Crust (page 17), unbaked

### For the Filling
454 g (16 oz) vegan cream cheese, room temperature

50 g (½ cup) powdered sugar

250 g (1½ cups) chopped vegan white chocolate (or chocolate chips), melted

96 g (1 cup) vegan whipped cream, room temperature

½ tsp pure vanilla extract

80 g (½ cup) vegan sprinkles

### For the Topping (optional)
40 g (¼ cup) vegan sprinkles

Preheat the oven to 325°F (165°C).

Make the Vegan Graham Crust. Bake the crust for 5 minutes, or until the crust is lightly toasted. Allow the crust to cool completely.

To make the filling, add the vegan cream cheese and powdered sugar to a bowl. With a stand mixer or hand mixer, whip the cream cheese and powdered sugar together for 1 minute, or until well incorporated. Add the melted vegan white chocolate, whipped cream and vanilla extract. Lightly mix until the ingredients are well combined, scraping the sides of the bowl as needed. Carefully fold in the vegan sprinkles.

Pour the filling into the cooled graham crust. Top the tart with additional sprinkles, if desired. Transfer the crust to the refrigerator and allow the tart to set for 30 minutes before serving.

# VEGAN SNICKERS® TART

## Yield: 1 (9" [23-cm]) tart

### For the Crust

125 g (1 cup) all-purpose flour

18 g (1½ tbsp) brown sugar

¼ tsp fine sea salt

75 g (½ cup) roasted peanuts

115 g (½ cup) unsalted vegan butter, cut into 1" (2.5-cm) cubes, cold

30–45 ml (2–3 tbsp) water

### For the Filling

340 g (1 cup) vegan caramel

113 g (¾ cup) roasted peanuts

### For the Topping

170 g (6 oz) chopped vegan dark chocolate (or chocolate chips)

32 g (2 tbsp) unsalted creamy peanut butter

1 tsp unrefined coconut oil

57 g (½ cup) roasted peanuts, chopped (optional)

I can trace my love for Snickers all the way back to childhood. They were my favorite chocolate bars, and after every Halloween, I would save all the Snickers bars and make them last as long as I could. This tart tastes just like a classic Snickers bar with a creamy vegan caramel filling and crunchiness from roasted peanuts, all enveloped in a peanut buttery chocolate topping.

Preheat the oven to 350°F (180°C).

To make the crust, add the flour, brown sugar, salt and peanuts to a food processor, and blend until the ingredients are well combined and crumbly. Add the vegan butter and pulse until the ingredients come together. Slowly add ½ tablespoon (7 ml) of water at a time until the crumbs come together when you pinch them.

Transfer the dough to a 9-inch (23-cm) tart pan, pressing on all sides until the pan is covered with the dough. Bake the crust for 10 to 12 minutes, or until it is lightly golden. Remove the crust from the oven and let it cool completely before adding the filling.

To make the filling, spread the vegan caramel across the bottom of the crust. Sprinkle the roasted peanuts evenly on top. Transfer the tart pan to the refrigerator for 25 minutes, or until the caramel has set.

To make the topping, add the chocolate, peanut butter and coconut oil to a glass bowl. Microwave in 15-second intervals until the chocolate starts to melt and you can stir all the ingredients together. Pour the mixture into the crust, spreading it evenly. Top the tart with the chopped roasted peanuts, if using.

Transfer the pan back to the refrigerator and allow the chocolate to set for 30 minutes before serving.

# VEGAN PEANUT BUTTER CUP TART

Yield: 1 (9" [23-cm]) tart

### For the Crust
1 Vegan Cookies and Cream Crust (page 18)

### For the Peanut Butter Filling
125 g (½ cup) unsalted creamy peanut butter

57 g (2 oz) vegan cream cheese, room temperature

115 g (1 cup + 3 tbsp) vegan whipped cream

### For the Chocolate Ganache
120 ml (½ cup) coconut cream

227 g (8 oz) chopped vegan dark chocolate (or chocolate chips)

### For the Topping
18 mini vegan peanut butter cups

Unsalted peanuts, chopped (optional)

We can't talk about childhood comfort food without mentioning Reese's® Peanut Butter Cups! They are one of my top-five favorite chocolate candies with their thick, sweet, peanut buttery filling wrapped up with a chocolate coating. Even writing this makes my stomach growl. If you love chocolate, peanut butter and, most importantly, Reese's, this recipe is for you! It tastes just like the original, but made vegan and with a cookies and cream crust!

---

Preheat the oven to 325°F (165°C).

Make the Vegan Cookies and Cream Crust. Bake for 5 minutes, or until the crust is lightly toasted. Allow the crust to cool completely.

To make the filling, add the peanut butter and vegan cream cheese to a bowl. Using a hand mixer, mix until the ingredients are well combined. Add the vegan whipped cream and carefully mix with a hand mixer, scraping down the sides as needed. Pour the filling into the crust. Transfer the tart to the refrigerator to set for 1 hour.

To make the chocolate ganache, add the coconut cream to a small saucepan and bring it to a simmer over medium heat. Place the chocolate in a heat-safe bowl. Pour the coconut cream over the chocolate and let it sit for 2 to 3 minutes. Mix the ingredients together with a spatula until it is smooth and creamy.

Pour the chocolate ganache over the tart, spreading it evenly. Transfer the tart back to the refrigerator and let it set for 30 minutes before serving, topped with the peanut butter cups and chopped peanuts, if using.

# CHOCOLATE BISCOFF®
# MOUSSE TART

## Yield: 1 (9" [23-cm]) tart

### For the Biscoff Crust
1 (250 g [8.8-oz]) package vegan Biscoff cookies

125 g (½ cup) unsalted creamy peanut butter

### For the Biscoff Layer
83 g (⅓ cup) vegan Biscoff butter or any vegan cookie butter

### For the Biscoff Filling
240 ml (1 cup) coconut cream

188 g (¾ cup) vegan Biscoff butter or any vegan cookie butter

28 g (2 tbsp) unsalted vegan butter

15 ml (1 tbsp) pure vanilla extract

255 g (9 oz) chopped vegan dark chocolate (or chocolate chips)

I first tasted Biscoff in its original cookie form at school. Growing up, there was not a lot of American food in my house. So, all the new foods I tried were often at school. I cannot tell you the joy I felt after the first bite of a Biscoff cookie, and even more, the first time I had Biscoff cookie butter. I couldn't stop eating it, couldn't stop thinking about it, and was obsessed with it for months. If you are a cookie butter fan, you know what I mean. This tart is not only vegan, but the filling is also rich and creamy, and the crust is made with Biscoff cookies. It is the perfect tart to make and have with your family, especially if you have little kids around.

---

Preheat the oven to 325°F (165°C).

To make the crust, add the Biscoff cookies to a food processor and pulse until you start seeing fine crumbs. Pour the crumbs into a bowl. Add the peanut butter and mix to combine. Transfer the crumbs to a pie or tart pan, pressing on all sides until the pan is covered with the cookie crumbs. Bake for 5 minutes, or until the crust is fragrant and lightly toasted. Let it cool completely.

To make the Biscoff layer, spread the Biscoff butter evenly over the bottom of the crust. Transfer the tart pan to the refrigerator to chill for 30 minutes.

To make the Biscoff filling, add the coconut cream, Biscoff butter, vegan butter and vanilla extract to a saucepan, and bring it to a boil over medium heat. Place the chocolate in a heat-safe bowl and pour the mixture over the chocolate. Allow the mixture to sit for 2 to 3 minutes. Mix all the ingredients together until smooth and creamy. Pour the filling into the crust. Transfer the pan back to the refrigerator and let it set for 2 to 3 hours or overnight.

# INDULGENT BLACK FOREST TART

## Yield: 1 (9" [23-cm]) tart

I first learned about Black Forest cake while watching a Chinese baking show. I remember being completely mesmerized by the chocolate and cherry layers and wanting nothing more than a slice to magically appear on my table. Whenever I am eating out and there is a Black Forest dessert, I almost always get it. This tart is not only indulgent, but it also combines a rich and decadent chocolate layer with fresh cherries.

### For the Chocolate Pastry Crust

156 g (1¼ cups) all-purpose flour

25 g (¼ cup) cacao powder

50 g (½ cup) powdered sugar

⅛ tsp fine sea salt

145 g (½ cup + 2 tbsp) unsalted vegan butter, cut into 1" (2.5-cm) cubes, cold

### For the Cherry Layer

75 g (½ cup) sliced fresh cherries

### For the Filling

313 ml (1¼ cups) full-fat coconut milk

150 g (1 cup) mashed fresh cherries

1 tsp pure vanilla extract

¼ tsp fine sea salt

¼ tsp agar-agar powder + 1 tsp cold water, combined

170 g (6 oz) chopped vegan dark chocolate (or chocolate chips)

### For the Topping (optional)

Vegan whipped cream

Fresh cherries

Preheat the oven to 350°F (180°C).

To make the crust, add the flour, cacao powder, powdered sugar and salt to a bowl, and mix with a spatula until well combined. Pour the mixture into a food processor and add the vegan butter. Pulse until a dough forms. Transfer the dough to a 9-inch (23-cm) tart pan, pressing on all the sides until the pan is covered with the crust. Bake for 15 minutes, or until lightly golden. Remove the crust from the oven and let it cool completely before adding the filling.

To make the cherry layer, add the sliced cherries to the bottom of the tart pan and set aside.

To make the filling, add the coconut milk, mashed cherries, vanilla extract and salt to a saucepan over medium heat, and simmer for 5 minutes. Pour the mixture through a strainer, and then bring the strained mixture back to a simmer. Add the agar-agar mixture and stir quickly. Place the chocolate in a heat-safe bowl, pour the coconut milk mixture over the chocolate and let it sit for 1 minute. Stir the ingredients together until smooth and creamy, scraping down the sides as needed. Pour the filling into the crust. Let it cool for 15 minutes before transferring it to the refrigerator to set for 2 to 3 hours or overnight. Top the tart with some vegan whipped cream and fresh cherries, if using, before serving!

# HOMEMADE VEGAN TWIX® TART

Yield: 1 (9" [23-cm]) tart

This tastes just like the real thing! When it comes to chocolate bars, Twix comes very close to number one for me. I love the balance of the vanilla shortbread with gooey caramel, all coated in chocolate. Well, this tart meets all of the above requirements and even more, as it's made with homemade vegan caramel that is healthier than the original non-vegan version! It will be loved by both kids and adults!

### For the Crust
1 Vegan Pastry Tart Crust (page 21)

### For the Caramel Layer
83 g (⅓ cup) unsalted almond butter

120 g (½ cup) unrefined coconut oil

170 ml (½ cup) maple syrup

¼ tsp fine sea salt

½ tsp pure vanilla extract

### For the Chocolate Ganache
120 ml (½ cup) coconut cream

227 g (8 oz) chopped vegan dark chocolate (or chocolate chips)

### For the Topping (optional)
Flaky sea salt

Make the Vegan Pastry Tart Crust and let it cool completely.

To make the caramel layer, add the almond butter, coconut oil, maple syrup, salt and vanilla extract to a saucepan, and bring it to a simmer over medium heat while stirring until smooth and creamy. Simmer for 15 to 20 minutes, or until the caramel thickens slightly, stirring the caramel constantly to prevent it from burning. Pour the caramel into the crust. Let it cool for 10 minutes before transferring it to the refrigerator to set for 30 minutes.

To make the ganache, add the coconut cream to a small saucepan and bring it to a simmer over medium heat. Place the chocolate in a heat-safe bowl, pour the coconut cream over the chocolate and let it sit for 2 to 3 minutes. Mix together until it is smooth and creamy. Pour the ganache into the tart, spreading it evenly. Transfer the tart back to the refrigerator and allow the ganache to set for 1 hour. Top the tart with some flaky sea salt, if using, before serving.

# GINGERBREAD SPICED MINI PIES

## Yield: 6 (3" [8-cm]) pies

When the holidays come around, you cannot miss having anything gingerbread related. On Christmas Day, I would wake up early in the morning and roll cookie dough to make gingerbread cookies. I could just sit in the kitchen all day enveloped with the smell of freshly baked gingerbread cookies. So naturally, I had to make a gingerbread spiced pie that is perfect for the holidays.

### For the Gingerbread Crust

75 g (⅓ cup) unsalted vegan butter, cut into 1" (2.5-cm) cubes, cold, plus more for greasing pans

208 g (1⅔ cups) all-purpose flour, plus more for dusting

50 g (½ cup) powdered sugar

6 g (2 tsp) ground cinnamon

1 tsp ground ginger

½ tsp ground nutmeg

¼ tsp ground allspice

⅛ tsp fine sea salt

10–15 ml (2–3 tsp) unsweetened plant-based milk of choice, cold

### For the Glaze

10 ml (½ tbsp) maple syrup

28 g (2 tbsp) unsalted vegan butter, melted

### For the Filling

1 (400-ml [1⅔ cups]) can full-fat coconut milk

120 g (¼ cup) molasses

1 tsp ground cinnamon

½ tsp ground ginger

¼ tsp ground nutmeg

⅛ tsp ground allspice

180 g (6 oz) chopped vegan dark chocolate (or chocolate chips)

### For the Topping (optional)

Fresh rosemary

Vegan whipped cream

Pomegranate seeds

Preheat the oven to 350°F (180°C). Grease six (3-inch [8-cm]) tart pans with vegan butter or coconut oil. Lightly flour a sheet of parchment paper.

To make the crust, add the flour, powdered sugar, cinnamon, ginger, nutmeg, allspice and salt in a food processor, and pulse to blend. Scatter the vegan butter over the flour and pulse until the butter is well incorporated. This should only take a few seconds. Add the plant-based milk 1 teaspoon at a time, pulsing with each addition. Stop adding the milk when you see soft, moist clumps. The dough is ready when you can pinch some dough and it holds together. Shape the dough into a disk. If the dough is still cold, you can roll out the dough now. If not, wrap the disk in plastic wrap or transfer it to an airtight container and refrigerate for 30 minutes.

Divide the dough into six equal pieces. Place one of the dough balls on the center of the floured parchment paper. Lightly flour the dough and cover it with a second sheet of parchment paper. Roll the dough into a circle that's 5 inches (13 cm) in diameter. Carefully transfer the dough to one of the pans; there should be some dough hanging over. Trim off the excess dough to a ¼-inch (6-mm) overhang. Fold the overhang dough under itself and pinch the crust to make a decorative edge. Repeat this step with the remaining dough. Transfer the pans to the freezer for 5 minutes.

To make the glaze, add the maple syrup and vegan butter to a small bowl, and mix well. Brush the crusts with the glaze. Add a sheet of parchment paper to the middle of each of the pie crusts and add pie weights or dried beans. Bake the crusts for 13 to 15 minutes, or until lightly golden. Remove the crusts from the oven and let them cool completely before adding the filling.

To make the filling, add the coconut milk, molasses, cinnamon, ginger, nutmeg and allspice to a saucepan, and bring it to a boil over medium heat. Stir until well combined. Place the chocolate in a heat-safe bowl, pour the boiling mixture over the chocolate and let it sit for 2 minutes. Stir with a spatula until smooth and creamy. Divide the filling into the prepared crusts. Let the mini pies cool for 5 minutes before transferring them to the refrigerator to chill for 2 hours or overnight. Before serving, top the tarts with some fresh rosemary, vegan whipped cream and pomegranate seeds, if using.

# PUMPKIN CARAMEL PIE

## Yield: 1 (9" [23-cm]) pie

### For the Crust
1 Classic Vegan Pie Crust (page 10)

### For the Filling
340 g (1 cup) vegan caramel
1 (425-g [15-oz]) can pumpkin puree
6 g (2 tsp) pumpkin pie spice
¼ tsp fine sea salt
40 g (¼ cup) cornstarch

### For the Topping (optional)
Vegan whipped cream
Chopped nuts of choice

When fall is in the air, it's nearly impossible to stop thinking about all the pumpkin desserts. Pumpkin pie is the first pie I ever baked for my family, and it remains one of my yearly must-makes for Thanksgiving. The pumpkin caramel filling in this pie is, without a doubt, one of the lightest and creamiest pumpkin pie fillings ever. It literally melts in your mouth! The filling combined with the buttery crust will leave you and your family wanting more!

Preheat the oven to 350°F (180°C).

Make the Classic Vegan Pie Crust and let it cool completely. Do not turn off the oven.

To make the filling, add the vegan caramel, pumpkin puree, pumpkin pie spice, salt and cornstarch to a bowl, and mix until well combined. Pour the filling into the crust. Bake for 25 minutes. You will know the filling is set when it looks darker and does not look as glossy as it was when it first went into the oven. Take the pie out of the oven and let it cool completely. Top the pie with some vegan whipped cream and chopped nuts, if using, before slicing.

# UNBELIEVABLY CREAMY NUTELLA® PIE

Yield: 1 (9" [23-cm]) pie

An indulgent and creamy Nutella pie that tastes just like the classic . . . but vegan! It is the epitome of decadence and makes for a wonderful dessert. The filling is smooth and rich, and with a chocolate graham crust—it will feel like you are eating a Nutella cookie. If you are a fan of chocolate and hazelnut, you will fall head over heels for this pie!

### For the Chocolate Graham Crust

155 g (15 full cracker sheets) vegan graham crackers

13 g (2 tbsp) cacao powder

⅛ tsp fine sea salt

60 g (¼ cup) unsalted vegan butter, melted

### For the Filling

188 ml (¾ cup) full-fat coconut milk

180 g (¾ cup) vegan chocolate hazelnut spread

1 tsp pure vanilla extract

⅛ tsp fine sea salt

227 g (8 oz) chopped vegan dark chocolate (or chocolate chips)

### For the Topping

Chopped hazelnuts or any other nuts of choice (optional)

Preheat the oven to 325°F (165°C).

To make the crust, place the graham crackers in a food processor and pulse until you start seeing fine crumbs. Add the cacao powder and salt, and pulse to combine. Pour the crumbs into a mixing bowl and add the vegan butter. Mix to combine. Transfer the crumbs to a 9-inch (23-cm) pie pan, pressing on all sides until the pan is covered with the graham crumbs. Bake for 5 minutes. Let it cool completely before adding the filling.

To make the filling, add the coconut milk, chocolate hazelnut spread, vanilla extract and salt to a saucepan, and bring it to a boil over medium heat, stirring until well combined. Place the chocolate in a heat-safe bowl. Pour the boiling mixture over the chocolate and let it sit for 2 minutes. Mix with a spatula until everything is well combined.

Pour the filling into the crust. Transfer the pan to the refrigerator and let it chill for at least 1 hour to set. Top the pie with chopped hazelnuts or other nuts, if using.

# VEGAN S'MORES PIE

**Yield: 1 (9" [23-cm]) pie**

### For the Crust
1 Vegan Graham Crust (page 17)

### For the Chocolate Ganache
240 g (1 cup) coconut cream

300 g (10.5 oz) chopped vegan dark chocolate (or chocolate chips)

### For the Topping
284 g (10 oz) vegan marshmallows

We cannot talk about comfort food without including s'mores! Don't worry though, you do not need a campfire to enjoy this classic combo of melty, gooey marshmallows and chocolate. This pie is made with a rich and fudgy chocolate filling, and topped with torched vegan marshmallows . . . perfect for those rainy and chilly days when you just want to be in your pj's all day. A slice of this pie will certainly bring back those childhood memories!

Preheat the oven to 325°F (165°C).

Make the Vegan Graham Crust. Bake the crust for 5 minutes and let it cool completely.

To make the ganache, add the coconut cream to a small saucepan and bring it to a simmer over medium heat. Place the chocolate in a heat-safe bowl. Once the coconut cream comes to a boil, pour it over the chocolate and let it sit for 2 to 3 minutes. Then, using a spatula, mix the ingredients together until it is smooth and creamy. Pour the ganache into the crust, spreading it evenly. Transfer the pie to the refrigerator and allow the chocolate ganache to set for 1 hour before serving. Top with the vegan marshmallows, and use a blow torch to brown the marshmallows before serving.

# PEANUT BUTTER AND JELLY HAND PIES

**Yield: 8 hand pies**

### For the Crust
1 Classic Vegan Pie Crust, unbaked (page 10)

All-purpose flour, for dusting

### For the Filling
80 g (¼ cup) strawberry jelly

63 g (¼ cup) unsalted creamy peanut butter

### For the Glaze
10 ml (½ tbsp) maple syrup

28 g (2 tbsp) unsalted vegan butter, melted

I don't think I know one person who doesn't like the classic combo of peanut butter and jelly. Because my mom doesn't know how to make American food, one of the very few American foods I had growing up was peanut butter and jelly sandwiches. We always had several jars of Skippy® peanut butter around and one large jar of strawberry jelly (my favorite) in our pantry. Whenever she did not want to cook, my mom would make us a tray of peanut butter and jelly sandwiches, placing it on our kitchen counter so that whoever was hungry could grab some. The gooey filling in these hand pies along with the flaky and buttery crust will just melt in your mouth, making you want to reach for another one!

Preheat the oven to 350°F (180°C). Line a baking sheet with parchment paper.

Make the Classic Vegan Pie Crust without baking it.

Lightly dust a clean surface with some flour. Roll the pie dough out into a circular shape that's 12 to 13 inches (30 to 33 cm) in diameter. Using a cookie cutter of choice (3 to 4 inches [8 to 10 cm]), cut the dough to your desired shape. Repeat the process until all the dough has been used.

Add 1 teaspoon of the strawberry jelly and 1 teaspoon of peanut butter to the center of one dough piece. (You can adjust the amount of the filling based on the size of your cookie cutter.) Top the filling with a second piece of dough. Crimp the edges together with a fork. Repeat this step until all the dough is used. Using a knife, cut 3 to 4 small lines in the top crust. Transfer the finished pies to the freezer for 5 minutes before baking.

To make the glaze, add the maple syrup and vegan butter to a small bowl, and mix well. Brush the pie crusts with the glaze. Bake for 20 minutes, or until the crust is golden. Remove the pies from the oven and let them cool for 5 to 10 minutes before serving.

# VEGAN GERMAN CHOCOLATE TART

## Yield: 1 (9" [23-cm]) tart

### For the Crust
1 Vegan Cookies and Cream Crust (page 18)

### For the Chocolate Ganache
240 g (1 cup) coconut cream

227 g (8 oz) chopped vegan dark chocolate (or chocolate chips)

### For the German Chocolate Topping
80 g (1 cup) unsweetened shredded coconut

95 g (½ cup) light brown sugar

¼ tsp fine sea salt

125 ml (½ cup) unsweetened plant-based milk of choice

60 g (¼ cup) unsalted vegan butter

1 tsp pure vanilla extract

10 g (1 tbsp) cornstarch + 15 ml (1 tbsp) water, combined

38 g (¼ cup) crushed pecans

I had German chocolate for the first time while I was in college. There was an Italian gelato store close to my college, and after every major exam, my friends and I would head over to get some gelato to celebrate. I tried their German chocolate gelato once and since then, I haven't been able to stop thinking about it. A bite of this tart instantly brings back memories of my college days. It is made with a layer of chocolate ganache filling and topped with coconut and pecans. Oh, did I mention it is also made with our Vegan Cookies and Cream Crust?

Preheat the oven to 325°F (165°C).

Make the Vegan Cookies and Cream Crust. Bake for 5 minutes and allow the crust to cool completely.

To make the ganache, add the coconut cream to a small saucepan and bring it to a boil over medium heat. Place the chocolate in a heat-safe bowl and pour the coconut cream over the chocolate. Let it sit for 2 to 3 minutes. Mix together until it is smooth and creamy. Pour the ganache into the crust, spreading it evenly. Transfer the tart back to the refrigerator and allow the chocolate ganache to set for about 1 hour.

To make the German chocolate topping, add the coconut, brown sugar and salt to a bowl, and mix until well combined. Place the plant-based milk, vegan butter and vanilla extract in a saucepan, and bring it to a simmer over medium heat. Pour the dry ingredients into the saucepan, stirring until everything is combined. Turn off the heat and add the cornstarch slurry, mixing everything together until the filling is well incorporated. Fold in the pecans. Pour the filling over the tart, spreading it evenly. Transfer the tart to the refrigerator for 30 minutes before serving.

# ASIAN-INSPIRED PIES AND TARTS

Nearly three decades ago, my mom landed in Boston Logan International Airport with only a few personal items.

Everything looked different and she didn't speak English. Women and men towered over her petite frame. She wanted to hop on the first airplane back to Vietnam, but she didn't. Instead, she courageously began a new life in America with my dad, navigating through a new country with each other.

Being one of the oldest among her siblings, my mom didn't have the chance to finish her education. When she immigrated to the United States, she had dreams and goals, but she decided to take another route and become a housewife. For her, the kitchen became her sanctuary.

So, I wrote this chapter to honor my culture, my parents and all the classic flavors I enjoyed growing up in an Asian household. You will find many Asian-inspired recipes here and some childhood classics such as Flaky, Buttery Chinese "Egg" Tarts (page 66), Creamy Ube Pie (page 61) and Classic Boba Tea Tartlets (page 62).

# STRAWBERRY MATCHA TART

## Yield: 1 (9" [23-cm]) tart

### For the Crust
1 Vegan Pastry Tart Crust (page 21)

### For the Matcha Filling
60 ml (¼ cup) water

6 g (1 tbsp) ceremonial-grade matcha powder

240 ml (1 cup) coconut cream

250 ml (1 cup) unsweetened plant-based milk of choice

50 g (½ cup) powdered sugar

1 tsp pure vanilla extract

1 tsp agar-agar powder + 10 ml (2 tsp) cold water, combined

### For the Topping
240 g (2 cups) fresh strawberries, sliced

If you asked me what my favorite fruit and drink is, my automatic response will be strawberries and matcha. There is nothing better than the taste of seasonal, ripe strawberries and a cup of matcha latte. So, you bet strawberry matcha is one of the first Asian-inspired tarts I want to share with you. This tart is made with a buttery crust along with a rich matcha cream filling and ripe, fresh strawberries. It is a combination your taste buds will thank you for, especially if you are a matcha lover!

Make the Vegan Pastry Tart Crust and let it cool completely.

To make the filling, heat the water either in a pot or a kettle. Remove it from the heat just before it boils. (If you use boiled water, the matcha will taste more bitter.) Sift the matcha into a small bowl. Pour the hot water into the bowl, and whisk back and forth in a zigzag motion with a bamboo whisk until no clumps are visible. If you don't have a bamboo whisk (although I highly recommend it, and it preserves the cultural aspect of matcha making!), you can also use a blender or milk frother—just make sure that all the matcha powder has dissolved. Set the matcha aside.

Add the coconut cream, plant-based milk, powdered sugar and vanilla extract to a saucepan and bring to a boil over medium heat, stirring to combine. Add the matcha and the agar-agar slurry, and stir for 1 minute.

Pour the filling into the crust and let it cool for 5 minutes before transferring it to the refrigerator for 3 hours to overnight, or until the filling sets. When ready to serve, top with the strawberries.

# CREAMY UBE PIE

Yield: 1 (9" [23-cm]) pie

Ube or purple yam, originating from the Philippines, is one of my mom's favorite snacks. Whenever we go to an Asian supermarket and she sees fresh ube, she buys a bag, steams them and snacks on them as she catches up with her favorite Chinese TV dramas. This pie is not only creamy and silky in texture, but the earthy flavor of the yam adds depth to the sweet, buttery filling.

## For the Crust
1 Classic Vegan Pie Crust (page 10)

## For the Filling
300 g (1 cup) mashed ube

250 ml (1 cup) unsweetened plant-based milk of choice

125 ml (~¼ cup + 2 tbsp) maple syrup

30 g (2 tbsp) unsalted vegan butter, melted

1 tsp pure vanilla extract

½ tsp ground cinnamon

¼ tsp fine sea salt

20 g (2 tbsp) cornstarch

Make the Classic Vegan Pie Crust and let it cool completely. Meanwhile, increase the oven temperature to 375°F (190°C).

To make the filling, add the mashed ube, plant-based milk, maple syrup, vegan butter, vanilla extract, ground cinnamon and salt to a bowl. Mix until all the ingredients are well combined, scraping down the sides of the bowl as needed. Add the cornstarch and mix well.

Pour the filling into the crust and bake for 30 minutes. You will know the filling is set when it looks darker and does not look as glossy as it was when it first went into the oven. Remove the pie from the oven and let it cool completely before slicing.

# CLASSIC BOBA TEA TARTLETS

Yield: 6 (3" [8-cm])
tartlets

I cannot talk about Asian-inspired flavors without mentioning boba tea! It is a classic drink I always had growing up. I could never get enough of the boba pearls. These cute boba tea tartlets are made with a classic Earl Grey custard filling and topped with boba pearls. It is a combination of silky filling and chewy topping.

### For the Crust

1 Classic Vegan Pie Crust, unbaked (page 10)

Vegan butter, for greasing pans

All-purpose flour, for dusting

### For the Glaze

10 ml (½ tbsp) maple syrup

28 g (2 tbsp) unsalted vegan butter, melted

### For the Earl Grey Custard Filling

240 ml (1 cup) coconut cream

207 ml (~¾ cup + 1 tbsp) unsweetened plant-based milk of choice

50 g (¼ cup) cane sugar

7 g (½ tbsp) unsalted vegan butter

15 ml (1 tbsp) pure vanilla extract

⅛ tsp fine sea salt

4 Earl Grey tea bags

20 g (2 tbsp) arrowroot powder + 30 ml (2 tbsp) cold water, combined

### For the Topping

120 g (1 cup) cooked tapioca pearls (boba pearls)

Preheat the oven to 350°F (180°C). Grease six (3-inch [8-cm]) pans with vegan butter or coconut oil. Lightly flour a sheet of parchment paper.

Make the Classic Vegan Pie Crust but don't bake it. Take the dough out of the refrigerator and divide it into six pieces. Place one of the pieces of dough on the center of the parchment paper. Lightly flour the dough and cover it with a second sheet of parchment paper. Roll the dough into a round shape that's 5 inches (13 cm) in diameter. Carefully transfer the dough to a greased pan. There should be some dough hanging over. Trim off the excess dough, leaving a ¼-inch (6-mm) overhang, and shape the edges with your hands, pressing on all the sides. Repeat this step with the remaining dough. Transfer the pans to the freezer for 5 minutes.

To make the glaze, add the maple syrup and vegan butter to a small bowl, and mix well. Brush the crusts with the glaze.

Add a sheet of parchment paper to the middle of the crusts and add pie weights or dried beans. Bake the crusts for 13 to 15 minutes, or until lightly golden. Allow the crusts to cool completely before adding the filling.

To make the filling, add the coconut cream, plant-based milk, sugar, vegan butter, vanilla extract and salt to a saucepan, and bring to a boil over medium heat. Immediately reduce the heat to low and add the Earl Grey tea bags. Allow the tea to steep for 10 minutes, then remove the tea bags from the saucepan. Bring the mixture back to a simmer. Pour in the arrowroot mixture, stirring quickly. Once the mixture starts to thicken, remove it from the heat and divide the filling among the tart pans. Allow the tarts to cool for 5 minutes before transferring them to the refrigerator to cool for 2 hours. Top with some of the tapioca pearls before serving.

# REFRESHING LYCHEE AND RASPBERRY TART

## Yield: 1 (9" [23-cm]) tart

### For the Crust
1 Vegan Oat Tart Crust (page 22)

### For the Filling
250 g (1 cup) canned lychee

63 g (½ cup) fresh raspberries

120 g (½ cup) coconut cream

1 tsp agar-agar powder + 10 ml (2 tsp) cold water, combined

### For the Topping (optional)
63 g (¼ cup) lychee (canned or fresh) or any other fruits of choice

Growing up, lychee was one of my favorite fruits. During the summer, my mom would buy a large bag of lychees from her weekly trips to Chinatown and put it in the refrigerator. Once they got cold, we would all huddle in the center of our kitchen, peeling away the skin of the lychees and eating our way through the entire bag. It was without a doubt one of the flavors I had to include in this chapter. This tart is made with my gluten-free Vegan Oat Tart Crust and filled with a refreshing lychee mixture that makes for the perfect summer dessert.

---

Make the Vegan Oat Tart Crust and let it cool completely.

To make the filling, add the lychee (with its water) and raspberries to a blender, and blend until smooth. Place a bowl under a strainer and pour the mixture through to remove any clumps. Add the mixture and the coconut cream to a saucepan, and bring it to a boil over medium heat. Add the agar-agar slurry to the saucepan, stirring all the ingredients for 1 minute, until the filling starts to thicken.

Pour the filling into the crust, and let it cool for 10 minutes. Transfer the tart to the refrigerator and let it cool for 2 hours or overnight. When ready to serve, top with additional lychee or any other fruit, if you want.

# FLAKY, BUTTERY CHINESE "EGG" TARTS

## Yield: 12 (2½" [6-cm]) tarts

You cannot walk into a Chinese bakery without getting a Chinese egg tart. It is one of the foods I missed the most when I went vegan . . . but fear no more. These egg tarts taste just like an authentic Chinese bakery's version, with a buttery and flaky crust filled with a sweet and creamy custard that will leave you reaching for another.

### For the Crust

Vegan butter, for greasing pans

All-purpose flour, for dusting

1 Classic Vegan Pie Crust, unbaked (page 10)

### For the Glaze

10 ml (½ tbsp) maple syrup

28 g (2 tbsp) unsalted vegan butter, melted

### For the Filling

500 ml (2 cups) unsweetened oat milk (or soy milk)

250 ml (1 cup) vegan evaporated milk

40 g (3 tbsp) vegan coconut custard powder

150 g (¾ cup) cane sugar

⅛ tsp kala namak salt (see Note)

Dash of turmeric powder (optional)

¾ tsp agar-agar powder + 8 ml (½ tbsp) cold water, combined

Preheat the oven to 350°F (180°C). Grease twelve (2½-inch [6-cm]) tartlet pans with vegan butter or coconut oil. Lightly flour a sheet of parchment paper.

Make the Classic Vegan Pie Crust but don't bake it. Take the dough out of the refrigerator and divide it into twelve pieces. Place one of the pieces of dough on the center of the parchment paper. Lightly flour it and cover with a second sheet of parchment paper. Roll the dough into a round shape that's 4 inches (10 cm) in diameter. Carefully transfer the dough into one of the buttered pans. There should be some dough hanging over. Trim off the excess dough to a ¼-inch (6-mm) overhang. Fold the overhang dough under itself and pinch the crust to make a decorative edge crust. Repeat this step with the remaining dough. Transfer the pans to the freezer for 5 minutes.

To make the glaze, add the maple syrup and vegan butter to a small bowl, and mix well. Brush the crusts with the glaze. Add a sheet of parchment paper to the middle of the pie crusts and add pie weights or dried beans. Bake for 13 to 15 minutes, or until lightly golden. Remove the crusts from the oven and let them cool completely before adding the filling.

To make the filling, add the oat milk, vegan evaporated milk, custard powder, cane sugar, kala namak salt and turmeric powder (if using) to a saucepan over medium heat. Whisk until all the ingredients are well combined and there are no lumps visible. Add the agar-agar slurry and stir for 1 minute, or until it starts to thicken slightly. Pour the filling into the crusts. Let them cool for 10 minutes before transferring them to the refrigerator to set for 2 hours or overnight.

Note: This is a must-have for the "eggy" taste of traditional Chinese egg tarts. It's also known as Himalayan black salt.

# PANDAN COCONUT TARTLETS

Yield: 12 (2½" [6-cm]) tartlets

Pandan is easily one of my favorite flavors. Growing up, my mom loved making pandan desserts. It has a sweet fragrance and a gorgeous, natural green color to it and is used in a lot of Asian recipes whether they be sweet or savory. These tartlets are made with a buttery, flaky crust, a silky, smooth pandan filling and toasted coconut flakes.

### For the Crust

Vegan butter, for greasing pans

All-purpose flour, for dusting

1 Classic Vegan Pie Crust, unbaked (page 10)

### For the Glaze

10 ml (½ tbsp) maple syrup

28 g (2 tbsp) unsalted vegan butter, melted

### For the Filling

500 ml (2 cups) unsweetened oat milk (or soy milk)

250 ml (1 cup) vegan evaporated milk

40 g (3 tbsp) vegan coconut custard powder

150 g (¾ cup) cane sugar

8 g (1½ tsp) pandan extract

¾ tsp agar-agar powder + 8 ml (½ tbsp) cold water, combined

### For the Topping

80 g (1 cup) shredded coconut, lightly toasted

Toasted coconut flakes (optional)

Preheat the oven to 350°F (180°C). Grease twelve (2½-inch [6-cm]) tartlet pans with vegan butter or coconut oil. Lightly flour a sheet of parchment paper.

Make the Classic Vegan Pie Crust but don't bake it. Take the dough out of the refrigerator and divide it into twelve pieces. Place one of the pieces of dough on the center of the parchment paper. Lightly flour it and cover it with a second sheet of parchment paper. Roll the dough into a round shape that's 4 inches (10 cm) in diameter. Carefully transfer the dough into one of the buttered pans. There should be some dough hanging over. Trim off the excess dough to a ¼-inch (6-mm) overhang. Fold the overhang dough under itself and pinch the crust to make a decorative edge crust. Repeat this step with the remaining dough. Transfer the pans to the freezer for 5 minutes.

To make the glaze, add the maple syrup and vegan butter to a small bowl, and mix well. Brush the crusts with the glaze. Add a sheet of parchment paper to the middle of the pie crusts and add pie weights or dried beans. Bake for 13 to 15 minutes, or until lightly golden. Remove the crusts from the oven and let them cool completely before adding the filling.

To make the filling, add the oat milk, vegan evaporated milk, custard powder, cane sugar and pandan extract to a saucepan, and bring to a boil over medium heat, whisking until well combined with no visible lumps. Turn off the heat, and add the agar-agar slurry. Stir for 1 minute. Pour the filling into the crusts. Let them cool for 10 minutes before transferring to the refrigerator to set for 2 hours or overnight. Top the tarts with the shredded coconut and coconut flakes, if using, before serving.

# MANDARIN ORANGE PANNA COTTA TART

Yield: 1 (9" [23-cm]) tart

### For the Crust
1 Vegan Pastry Tart Crust (page 21)

### For the Filling
240 ml (1 cup) fresh mandarin orange juice

180 ml (¾ cup) coconut cream

83 ml (⅓ cup) unsweetened plant-based milk of choice

100 g (½ cup) cane sugar

1 tsp pure vanilla extract

35 g (3½ tbsp) cornstarch + 45 ml (3 tbsp) cold water, combined

### For the Topping (optional)
Fresh mandarin oranges, peeled

My mom loved buying mandarin oranges, especially during the Chinese holidays. For one, they last longer than other fruits, and two, they are an important symbol of the Chinese New Year, symbolizing abundance and happiness. So, every year, when it came time to celebrate Chinese New Year, our entire refrigerator would be filled with mandarin oranges. We would still be eating them months later, and I would always try to make something out of them . . . like this tart. The filling bursts with citrus flavors; it's not overly sweet; and it balances well with a buttery crust.

Make the Vegan Pastry Tart Crust and let it cool completely.

To make the filling, add the mandarin orange juice, coconut cream, plant-based milk, sugar and vanilla extract to a saucepan, and bring to a boil over medium heat. Add the cornstarch slurry to the saucepan, stirring all the ingredients quickly together. Turn off the heat after 10 to 15 seconds, or once the filling starts to thicken.

Pour the filling into the crust. Let it cool for 5 minutes before transferring it to the refrigerator to set for 3 hours or overnight. When ready to serve, top the tart with mandarin oranges, if desired.

# VIETNAMESE COFFEE PANNA COTTA PIE

Yield: 1 (9" [23-cm]) pie

### For the Crust
1 Classic Vegan Pie Crust (page 10)

### For the Filling
120 ml (¾ cup) coconut cream

125 ml (½ cup) unsweetened plant-based milk of choice

120 ml (½ cup) vegan condensed coconut milk

6 g (2 tsp) agar-agar powder + 30 ml (2 tbsp) cold water, combined and divided

240 ml (1 cup) freshly brewed Vietnamese coffee (I used Café du Monde)

### For the Coffee Syrup
120 ml (½ cup) freshly brewed Vietnamese coffee

85 g (~½ cup) brown sugar

My mom is absolutely obsessed with coffee, but not just any coffee. It has to be Vietnamese coffee. She has a cup every morning, and if she goes a day without it, she's in the worst mood and you would not want to talk to her. If you are not familiar, Vietnamese coffee is made with dark roast coffee (I like to use Café du Monde® ground coffee) mixed with sweetened condensed milk. Vietnamese coffee is becoming more and more popular, but the Vietnamese coffee brands I suggest include Trung Nguyen, Vinacafé, Chestbrew and Lang Thang. This pie combines a buttery crust with layers of creamy vegan condensed coconut milk and a strong coffee layer, topped with a homemade coffee syrup.

Make the Classic Vegan Pie Crust and let it cool completely.

To make the filling, add the coconut cream, plant-based milk and condensed coconut milk to a saucepan, and bring to a simmer over medium heat. Reduce the heat to low. Remove 125 grams (½ cup) of the mixture and place it in a separate, smaller saucepan over medium-low heat. This will be the condensed milk layer. Add 12 grams (1 tablespoon) of the agar-agar mixture to the smaller saucepan and bring it to a simmer for 1 minute, stirring constantly. Transfer the mixture to the pie crust. Allow the mixture to cool for 5 minutes before transferring the pie to the refrigerator for 20 minutes to chill and set.

To the larger saucepan, add the coffee and bring it to a boil. Add the remaining agar-agar mixture, and bring it to a simmer for 1 minute, stirring constantly. Allow the mixture to cool for 3 minutes before adding it to the top of the condensed milk layer. Transfer the pie back to the refrigerator to chill for 1 hour, or until the filling sets.

To make the coffee syrup, add the coffee and brown sugar to a saucepan over medium-low heat. Stir constantly until it begins to thicken slightly, about 1 minute. Remove from the heat to cool completely. Drizzle the syrup over the pie when you're ready to serve.

# CHINESE WHITE PEAR AND GINGER PIE

## Yield: 1 (9" [23-cm]) tart

### For the Crust
2 Classic Vegan Pie Crusts (page 10), 1 par-baked and the other unbaked

All-purpose flour, for dusting

### For the Pears
600 g (6 medium) Chinese white pears, unpeeled and sliced thinly

100 g (½ cup) cane sugar

### For the Filling
50 g (¼ cup) cane sugar, divided

1 tsp grated fresh ginger

½ tsp ground cinnamon

¼ tsp ground nutmeg

20 g (2 tbsp) arrowroot powder

28 g (2 tbsp) unsalted vegan butter, cut into 1" (2.5-cm) cubes, cold

### For the Glaze
10 ml (½ tbsp) maple syrup

28 g (2 tbsp) unsalted vegan butter, melted

38 g (3 tbsp) cane sugar

I grew up with several large pear trees around my house. Every fall, we would harvest baskets and baskets of pears of different varieties, meaning we wouldn't have to buy any fruit for months. The one exception was Chinese white pears, which we couldn't grow. They are so juicy and sweet that we couldn't resist buying them. Even my siblings, who do not like fruit, would eat these. This pie is made with a double, flaky pie crust combined with Chinese white pears and warming spices, making it the perfect fall dessert!

---

Make 2 Classic Vegan Pie Crusts, but only par-bake one of them. Leave the oven on and increase the temperature to 400°F (205°C). Lightly flour a sheet of parchment paper.

For the pears, add the pears and sugar to a bowl, and mix well. Set aside for 30 minutes to allow some of the juices from the pears to come out, preventing a soggy-bottom crust.

For the crust, set aside the par-baked crust for the bottom of the pie. Use the unbaked crust for the top by taking the dough out of the refrigerator and placing it on the center of the floured parchment paper. Lightly flour the dough and cover it with a second sheet of parchment paper. Roll the dough into a round shape that's 12 inches (30 cm) in diameter. Set aside.

For the filling, transfer the pears to a separate bowl, leaving the juices behind. Add the sugar, ginger, cinnamon, nutmeg and arrowroot powder. Toss until all the ingredients are combined. Pour the filling into the par-baked crust. Sprinkle the butter over the pears. Place the rolled crust over the pears and lightly press the rim against the edges of the bottom crust. Cut slits in the top crust.

To make the glaze, add the maple syrup and vegan butter to a small bowl, and mix well. Brush the top crust with the glaze, and then top with the cane sugar.

Bake the pie on the middle rack for 15 minutes, and then reduce the temperature to 350°F (180°C). Bake for 30 minutes. If the crust starts to brown, cover it with a loose piece of aluminum foil. You will know the pie is done when the crust is golden brown and the pear juice is bubbling up through the top-crust slits. Transfer the pie to a wire rack and let it cool until it reaches room temperature before slicing. The cooling time is important to allow the filling to set.

# BLACK SESAME TOTORO TARTLETS

### Yield: 6 (3" [8-cm]) tartlets

These tartlets are absolutely a joy to make! Nutty in taste, they are reminiscent of peanut butter! Did I also mention that this cute Totoro-shaped topping brings back childhood memories of watching the movie *My Neighbor Totoro*?

### For the Crust
1 Vegan Pastry Tart Crust, unbaked (page 21)

### For the Glaze
10 ml (½ tbsp) maple syrup
28 g (2 tbsp) unsalted vegan butter, melted

### For the Black Sesame Filling
25 g (2½ tbsp) toasted black sesame seeds
6 g (½ tbsp) cane sugar
250 ml (1 cup) unsweetened plant-based milk of choice
180 ml (¾ cup) coconut cream
85 g (¼ cup) maple syrup
½ tsp agar-agar powder + 1 tsp cold water, combined

### For the Topping
72 g (¾ cup) vegan whipped cream
32 g (~1 oz) chopped vegan dark chocolate (or chocolate chips), melted
Fresh mint leaves

Preheat the oven to 375°F (190°C).

Prepare the Vegan Pastry Tart Crust. Transfer the dough to six (3-inch [8-cm]) tart pans, pressing on all sides until the pans are covered with the dough.

To make the glaze, add the maple syrup and vegan butter to a small bowl, and mix well. Brush the dough with the glaze. Add a sheet of parchment paper to the middle of the dough and add pie weights or dried beans. Bake for 8 to 10 minutes, or until lightly golden. Remove the crusts from the oven and let them cool completely before adding the filling.

To make the black sesame filling, add the sesame seeds and sugar to a food processor, and process until the sesame seeds become a powder. Add the plant-based milk, coconut cream and maple syrup to a saucepan, and bring to a boil over medium heat. Add the sesame seed powder. Allow the mixture to simmer for 5 minutes, or until the mixture turns a grayish color. Carefully pour the mixture through a sieve to remove any seeds, then return it to the saucepan and bring it to a boil. Slowly add the agar-agar slurry, stirring constantly for 1 minute. Turn off the heat and pour the filling into the tart crusts. Allow the filling to cool for 10 minutes before transferring them to the refrigerator to chill for 2 to 3 hours.

To make the topping (Totoro face), with a hand mixer, whip the vegan whipped cream until smooth and creamy. Add the whipped cream to a piping bag. Make a half-dome shape on one of the tarts and top with a pair of eyes. Using the melted chocolate, add the pupils, whiskers and nose. Top with a mint leaf on the top of the face. Repeat with the remaining tarts.

# FRUIT-FORWARD FLAVORS

When I was growing up, outside my house felt like a mini forest as it was almost always covered with our large peach and pear trees. If you looked at it from an angle, you wouldn't even be able to see the house, especially during the summer months when all the plants were in full bloom. We loved to shop at farmers' markets, and we also grew our own vegetables and fruits whenever we could. Each spring, my mom and I would set out to purchase new seeds to plant our garden, and I am still blown away by how seeds transform into tomatoes, cucumbers and berries.

So, it's no surprise that this chapter is inspired by these childhood memories and what we grew in our garden, such as strawberries for a refreshing Strawberry Yogurt Tart (page 80), peaches for my Peaches and Cream Tartlets (page 83) and lemons for some Tangy Earl Grey Lemon Tartlets (page 84) . . . all plant-based and made with simple ingredients. I am actually allergic to apples, so you will not see any apple recipes here, but you will find an array of fruit-based recipes such as adorable Cherry Pie Pops (page 92) that are loved by adults and children alike. I hope you will enjoy these naturally flavored treats with your loved ones or by yourself!

# STRAWBERRY YOGURT TART

## Yield: 1 (9" [23-cm]) tart

### For the Crust
1 Vegan Pastry Tart Crust (page 21)

### For the Filling
250 ml (1 cup) unsweetened plant-based milk of choice

340 g (~1 cup + 7 ½ tbsp) unsweetened plant-based yogurt

113 ml (⅓ cup) maple syrup

1 tsp agar-agar powder + 10 ml (2 tsp) cold water, combined

### For the Topping
120 g (1 cup) fresh strawberries, stems removed and sliced

85 ml (¼ cup) maple syrup

If you know anything about me, you know that I am obsessed with strawberries. I look forward to this fruit the most when spring and summer come around. When I was little, my parents would buy cases and cases of fresh strawberries at the farmers' market, and I would eat them all in less than a week. Without a doubt, strawberries are a highlight in this cookbook and especially this chapter. This tart is made with a creamy and silky filling that is not overly sweet and topped with fresh, ripe strawberries that make for the perfect snack or dessert for spring and summer!

Make the Vegan Pastry Tart Crust and allow the crust to cool completely.

To make the filling, add the plant-based milk, plant-based yogurt and maple syrup to a saucepan over medium heat. Stir until all the ingredients are combined and the filling starts to simmer. Slowly add the agar-agar slurry, stirring constantly for 1 minute. Turn off the heat and pour the filling into the tart crust. Allow the filling to cool for 10 minutes before transferring it to the refrigerator to chill for 2 to 3 hours. When ready to serve, top the crust with the sliced strawberries, and then brush the strawberries with the maple syrup.

# PEACHES AND CREAM TARTLETS

Yield: 6 (3" [8-cm]) tartlets

Growing up, there was a large peach tree in our yard. Every summer, my parents would put out a ladder and let me climb to the top to pick the ripest peaches at the peak season. I couldn't stop smiling when I got the biggest and ripest peaches and would show them to my parents like I won a trophy. Biting into one instantly makes me feel like I am in heaven, and these tartlets make me feel the same way with their fresh, sweet and creamy filling . . . making me wish summer would never end!

### For the Crust
1 Vegan Pastry Tart Crust, unbaked (page 21)

### For the Filling
163 g (1¼ cups) raw cashews, soaked in water overnight

300 g (2–3 large) ripe peaches, peeled and sliced thinly

100 g (⅓ cup + 4 tsp) coconut cream

113 ml (⅓ cup) maple syrup

40 ml (2 tbsp + 2 tsp) fresh lemon juice

Zest of 1 lemon

10 g (1 tbsp) arrowroot powder

1 tsp pure vanilla extract

Dash of turmeric powder (optional, for color)

### For the Topping (optional)
Sliced fresh peaches and any other fruit of choice

Preheat the oven to 375°F (190°C).

Make the Vegan Pastry Tart Crust. Transfer the dough to six (3-inch [8-cm]) tartlet pans, pressing on all sides until the pans are covered with the dough. Bake the crusts for 8 to 10 minutes, or until lightly golden. Remove the crusts from the oven and let them cool completely before adding the filling.

To make the filling, drain the soaked cashews. Add the cashews, peaches, coconut cream, maple syrup, lemon juice, lemon zest, arrowroot powder, vanilla extract and turmeric powder (if using) to a food processor and blend until all the ingredients are smooth, scraping down the sides as needed. Divide the filling between the tart pans. Transfer the pans to the refrigerator to chill for 3 hours or overnight. When the tartlets are ready, top with sliced, fresh peaches and any other fruits (if using).

# TANGY EARL GREY LEMON TARTLETS

Yield: 6 (3" [8-cm]) tartlets

This is one dessert that will always stand out in my memory as one of the most delicious I've had. The shortbread crust is infused with coconut flavors. The filling is smooth, creamy and refreshing with tangy lemon flavors and steeped with that floral, bergamot taste from the tea. These will be an absolute hit for all lemon and tea lovers!

### For the Crust

150 g (1½ cups) almond flour

32 g (~6 tbsp) unsweetened shredded coconut

25 g (¼ cup) powdered sugar

⅛ tsp fine sea salt

15 g (1 tbsp) unrefined coconut oil, melted

1 tsp pure vanilla extract

### For the Filling

1 (400-ml [13.5-fl oz]) can coconut cream

240 ml (1 cup) fresh lemon juice

Zest of 1 lemon

50 g (½ cup) powdered sugar

2 Earl Grey tea bags

20 g (2 tbsp) arrowroot powder

1 tsp agar-agar powder

30 ml (2 tbsp) cold water

### For the Topping (optional)

Fresh fruit or edible flowers of choice

Preheat the oven to 350°F (180°C).

To make the crust, add the almond flour, shredded coconut, powdered sugar and salt to a bowl, and mix until all the ingredients are combined. Add the coconut oil and vanilla extract, and mix until the dough comes together. Divide the dough among six (3-inch [8-cm]) tartlet pans, pressing on the bottoms and sides. Bake the crusts for 12 to 15 minutes, or until they are lightly golden.

To make the filling, add the coconut cream, lemon juice, lemon zest and powdered sugar to a saucepan, and bring to a simmer over medium heat. Add the Earl Grey tea bags, turn off the heat and steep for 20 minutes. Remove the tea bags and bring the filling back to a simmer.

Add the arrowroot powder, agar-agar powder and water to a bowl, and mix until they are well combined. Slowly pour the arrowroot mixture into the saucepan and whisk until combined. When it starts to thicken, 15 to 20 seconds, turn off the heat and pour the filling through a sieve over a bowl to allow for a smoother texture. Divide the filling among the crusts. Place the tarts in the refrigerator to set for at least 4 hours or overnight. When ready to serve, top with any fresh fruits or edible flowers (if using).

# BANANA CARAMEL TART

## Yield: 1 (9" [23-cm]) tart

### For the Crust
1 Vegan Pastry Tart Crust (page 21)

### For the Filling
150 g (¾ cup) Medjool dates, soaked in water overnight

180 g (1½ medium) ripe bananas, sliced thinly

30 g (2 tbsp) unrefined coconut oil, melted

60 ml (¼ cup) hot water

1 tsp pure vanilla extract

¼ tsp fine sea salt

### For the Topping (optional)
Sliced fresh bananas

Chopped nuts

Melted vegan chocolate

Since I was little, I've always eaten bananas. Not just any bananas though. They have to be slightly green and just starting to ripen. If there are any ripe bananas in my kitchen, my first reaction is to make banana bread or some other banana dessert with them, which led to this tart. It tastes just like the classic banana cream pie, but this version is naturally sweetened with Medjool dates.

---

Make the Vegan Pastry Tart Crust and let it cool completely.

To make the filling, drain the soaked dates and add the dates, bananas, coconut oil, hot water, vanilla extract and salt to a food processor, and blend until it is completely smooth and creamy, scraping down the sides as needed. Pour the filling into the crust, smoothing the top. Transfer the tart to the refrigerator to set for 3 hours or overnight. When the tart is ready, top it with sliced bananas, chopped nuts and a drizzle of melted chocolate (if using).

# CHAMOMILE GRAPEFRUIT TART

## Yield: 1 (9" [23-cm]) tart

### For the Crust
1 Vegan Pastry Tart Crust (page 21)

### For the Filling
1 (400-ml [13.5-fl oz]) can coconut cream

240 ml (1 cup) fresh grapefruit juice

75 g (¾ cup) powdered sugar

1 tsp pure vanilla extract

2 chamomile tea bags

20 g (2 tbsp) arrowroot powder

1 tsp agar-agar powder

30 ml (2 tbsp) cold water

### For the Topping (optional)
Peeled grapefruit or any other fruit of choice

Nothing brings me more joy than seeing the bursting colors of citrus during those cold and gloomy winter days. This grapefruit tart features a creamy, smooth custard filling made with fresh grapefruit juice, depths of citrus flavors with hints of acidity to it and a touch of chamomile flavors and floral sweetness from the infused chamomile tea. If this doesn't convince you to have a slice, the color certainly will win you over!

Make the Vegan Pastry Tart Crust and let it cool completely.

To make the filling, add the coconut cream, grapefruit juice, powdered sugar and vanilla extract to a saucepan, and bring to a boil over medium heat. Add the chamomile tea bags, turn off the heat and steep for 15 minutes. Remove the tea bags and bring the filling back to a simmer.

Add the arrowroot powder, agar-agar powder and cold water to a bowl, and mix until they are well combined. Slowly pour the arrowroot mixture into the saucepan and whisk until combined. When it starts to thicken, about 30 seconds, turn off the heat and pour the filling through a sieve over a bowl to allow for a smoother texture. Pour the filling into the crust and let it cool for 10 minutes before transferring it to the refrigerator to set for 3 hours or overnight. Top with the peeled grapefruit or other fruit (if using) when ready to serve.

# CHERRY WHITE CHOCOLATE TART

## Yield: 1 (9" [23-cm]) tart

### For the Crust
1 Vegan Oat Tart Crust (page 22)

### For the Cherry Filling
300 g (2 cups) pitted cherries

240 ml (1 cup) water

85 ml (¼ cup) maple syrup

1 tsp pure vanilla extract

1 tsp agar-agar powder + 2 tsp (10 ml) cold water, combined

### For the White Chocolate Layer
98 g (¾ cup) raw cashews, soaked in water overnight, drained

120 ml (½ cup) coconut cream

45 g (3½ tbsp) cane sugar

30 g (2 tbsp) unrefined coconut oil, melted

57 g (2 oz) chopped vegan white chocolate (or chocolate chips)

### For the Topping (optional)
Additional fresh cherries and any other fruit of choice

Unsweetened coconut flakes

We did have one cherry tree in our garden, but it only lasted a few years. Its sweet fragrance naturally attracted bees so we had to race to pick all the cherries before the bees got to them. There was always a 50 percent chance that any of our cherries would be absolutely sour. Don't worry though, because this tart is sure to be sweet, as it's made with fresh, ripe cherries layered with a creamy vegan white chocolate layer and a gluten-free oat crust.

Make the Vegan Oat Tart Crust and let it cool completely.

To make the cherry filling, add the cherries and water to a food processor, and blend until smooth. Pour the mixture into a saucepan over medium heat. Add the maple syrup and vanilla extract. Mix well and bring to a simmer. Add the agar-agar slurry and stir constantly. Once the filling starts to thicken slightly, 15 to 20 seconds, pour it into the crust and let it cool for 5 minutes before transferring it to the refrigerator to set for 1 hour.

To make the white chocolate layer, add the cashews and coconut cream to a food processor, and blend until the cashews are smooth and creamy. Transfer the mixture to a saucepan over medium-low heat. Add the sugar and coconut oil, and stir until all the ingredients are well combined. When the filling begins to simmer, turn off the heat and add the white chocolate. Allow the filling to sit for 1 minute, and then mix until the white chocolate is well combined.

Pour the filling over the cherry layer in the crust. Allow the tart to cool for 10 minutes before transferring it to the refrigerator to set for 2 hours or overnight. When the tart is ready, top with the additional cherries, other fruits and coconut flakes (if using).

# CHERRY PIE POPS

### Yield: 12 pie pops

There were always bake sales at the elementary school I went to. Other than cookies, one of the baked goods I looked forward to the most was pie pops. Not only because I love pies, but they look absolutely adorable in mini sizes on a pop stick. These pie pops are made with a classic flaky and buttery crust along with a fresh, homemade cherry filling. With the cute shapes and great taste, these will be a favorite among children and adults alike!

### For the Crust
1 Classic Vegan Pie Crust, unbaked (page 10)

All-purpose flour, for dusting

### For the Cherry Filling
200 g (1⅓ cups) pitted cherries

43 g (¼ cup) brown sugar

8 ml (½ tbsp) fresh lemon juice

Dash of ground cinnamon

10 g (1 tbsp) arrowroot powder

### For the Glaze
10 ml (½ tbsp) maple syrup

28 g (2 tbsp) unsalted vegan butter, melted

Preheat the oven to 350°F (180°C). Line a baking sheet with parchment paper.

Make the Classic Vegan Pie Crust without baking it. Set the dough aside.

To make the cherry filling, add the cherries, brown sugar, lemon juice and cinnamon to a saucepan, and bring to a simmer over medium-low heat. Once the cherries have broken apart, slowly add the arrowroot powder, stirring quickly. When the filling begins to thicken, after 10 to 15 seconds, turn off the heat and transfer the filling to a bowl to cool completely.

Lightly dust a clean surface with some flour. Roll out the dough to a circular shape that's 12 to 13 inches (30 to 33 cm) in diameter. Using your cookie cutter of choice (1½ to 2 inches [4 to 5 cm] wide), cut the dough to your desired shape. Repeat until all the dough has been used. You should have 24 pieces.

Add 7 grams (1 teaspoon) of the cherry filling to the center of one piece of cut-out dough. You can also adjust the amount of the filling based on the size of your cookie cutters, if needed. Place a cake pop stick in the center of the filling. Top with a second piece of cut-out dough. Use a fork to crimp the edges together. Repeat this step until all the dough is used. Transfer the finished pies to the freezer for 5 minutes, then bake the pies for 15 to 18 minutes, or until the crusts are golden. Remove the pies from the oven and let them cool for 5 to 10 minutes.

To make the glaze, add the maple syrup and vegan butter to a small bowl, and mix well. Brush the cherry pies with the glaze when you're ready to serve.

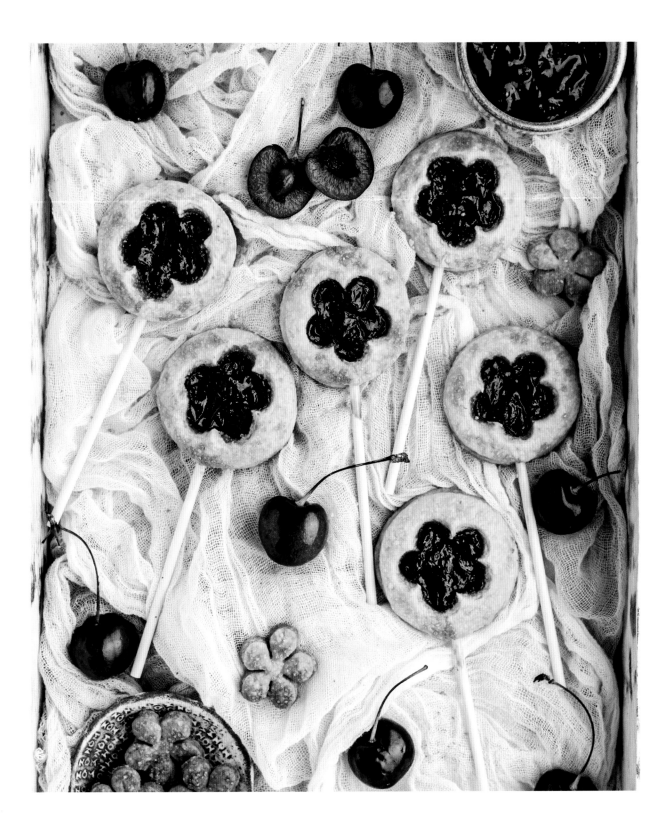

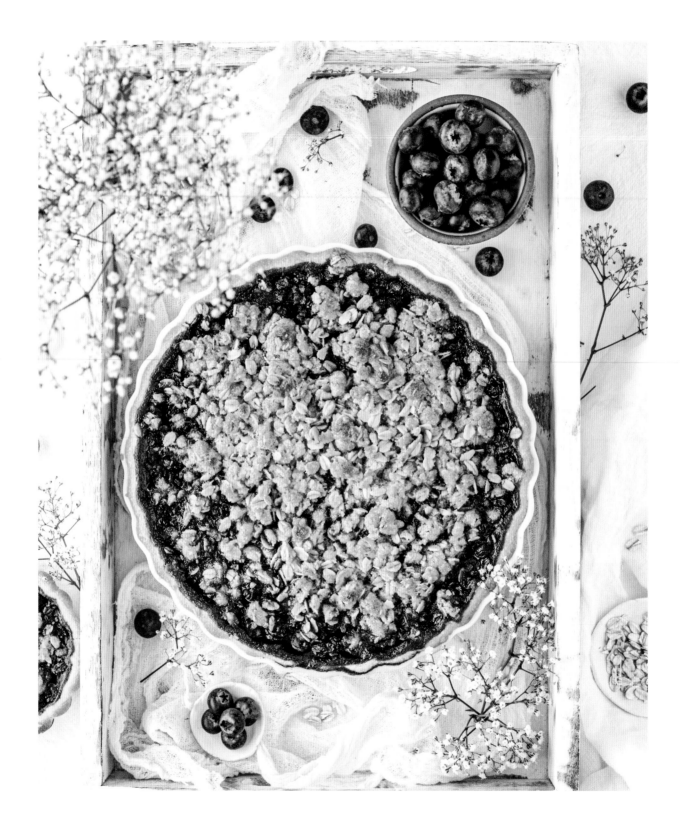

# BLUEBERRY CRUMBLE PIE

Yield: 1 (9" [23-cm]) pie

### For the Crust
1 Classic Vegan Pie Crust (page 10)

### For the Crumble Topping
80 g (⅓ cup) rolled oats

42 g (⅓ cup) all-purpose flour

100 g (½ cup) cane sugar

1 tsp ground cinnamon

84 g (6 tbsp) unsalted vegan butter, cut into 1" (2.5-cm) cubes, cold

### For the Filling
600 g (4 cups) fresh blueberries

100 g (½ cup) cane sugar

15 ml (1 tbsp) fresh lemon juice

Zest of 1 lemon

⅛ tsp fine sea salt

35 g (4½ tbsp) tapioca flour

Vegan vanilla ice cream or other vegan ice cream of choice (optional, for serving)

What can I say about this pie? It truly is my favorite pie of all time. As mentioned in the introduction, I was in the hospital for a few months when I was fourteen years old because of an eating disorder. While at the hospital, the first dessert I allowed myself to eat was blueberry pie. I know many do not think that hospital food is good, but at that time, and to this day, it was the best blueberry pie I've ever had. And it's the reason blueberry pie will always be my favorite. This recipe is an ode to the vulnerable, teenage version of me as well as the me today. This pie is made with a flaky crust and loaded with fresh, sweet and juicy blueberries and an oat crumble topping. You won't be able to resist a second slice. I promise!

---

Make the Classic Vegan Pie Crust and let it cool completely. Keep the oven on and increase the temperature to 400°F (205°C).

To make the crumble topping, add the oats, flour, sugar and cinnamon to a bowl, and mix until well combined. Add the vegan butter and mix until a crumble forms. It should resemble cookie dough. Set the crumble in the refrigerator while you make the filling.

To make the filling, add the blueberries, sugar, lemon juice, lemon zest, salt and tapioca flour to a bowl. Carefully toss all the ingredients together. Pour the filling into the pie crust.

Sprinkle the crumble topping over the blueberry layer. Bake for 15 minutes, and then reduce the oven temperature to 375°F (190°C). Bake for 25 to 30 minutes, or until the blueberries are bursting with their juices.

Allow the pie to cool for 20 minutes before serving with vanilla ice cream, if using.

# SWEET POTATO MISO PIE WITH CHOCOLATE CRUST

### Yield: 1 (9" [23-cm]) pie

### For the Crust

220 g (1¾ cups) all-purpose flour, plus more for dusting

145 g (½ cup + 2 tbsp) unsalted vegan butter, cut into 1" (2.5-cm) cubes, cold, plus more for greasing pan

30 g (¼ cup + ½ tsp) cacao powder

50 g (½ cup) powdered sugar

½ tsp fine sea salt

5–10 ml (1–2 tsp) unsweetened plant-based milk of choice, cold

### For the Glaze

10 ml (½ tbsp) maple syrup

28 g (2 tbsp) unsalted vegan butter, melted

### For the Filling

600 g (2 cups) sweet potato puree

125 ml (½ cup) full-fat coconut milk

85 ml (¼ cup) maple syrup

30 g (2 tbsp) white miso paste

20 g (2 tbsp) cornstarch

⅛ tsp fine sea salt

Oh, sweet potatoes! Available in the United States year-round, I still look forward to sweet potatoes the most when autumn arrives. This is not your traditional sweet potato pie, but one made with a chocolate crust and a rich, creamy sweet potato filling that's light and airy due to the addition of miso paste.

Preheat the oven to 350°F (180°C). Lightly flour a sheet of parchment paper. Grease a 9-inch (23-cm) pie pan with vegan butter or coconut oil.

To make the crust, combine the flour, cacao powder, powdered sugar and salt in a food processor, and pulse to blend. Scatter the butter over the flour and pulse until the butter is well incorporated. This should only take a few seconds. Add the plant-based milk 1 teaspoon at a time and pulse with each addition. Stop adding the milk when you see soft, moist clumps. The dough is ready when you pinch some dough and it holds together.

Shape the dough into a disk. If the dough is still cold, you can roll out the dough. If not, wrap the disk in plastic wrap or transfer it to an airtight container and refrigerate for 30 minutes. Place the dough in the center of the floured parchment paper. Lightly flour the dough and cover it with a second sheet of parchment paper. Roll the dough into a round shape that's 12 inches (30 cm) in diameter. Carefully transfer the dough to the greased pie pan. There should be some dough hanging over. Trim off the dough and shape the edges with your hands, pressing on all the sides. Transfer the crust to the freezer for 5 minutes.

To make the glaze, add the maple syrup and vegan butter to a small bowl, and mix well. Brush the crust with the glaze. Add a sheet of parchment paper to the middle of the dough and add pie weights or dried beans. Bake for 13 to 15 minutes, or until the crust is slightly darker in color. Let it cool completely. Do not turn off the oven.

To make the filling, add the sweet potatoes, coconut milk, syrup, miso paste, cornstarch and salt to a bowl, and mix until all the ingredients are well combined. Pour the filling into the pie crust, smoothing the top.

Bake for 35 minutes. You will know the filling is set when it looks darker and does not look as glossy as it was when it first went into the oven. Remove the pie from the oven and let it cool for 20 minutes before slicing.

# FORGET THE OVEN! NO-BAKE TARTS

I am a baker at heart, but there are times when I absolutely do not want to turn on the oven, especially during those boiling hot and humid summer days. I do not want to make my apartment even hotter with the oven on, and I certainly do not want to be sweating all day (although I would make an exception if I was on vacation somewhere tropical). So, I always have a few recipes on hand that require no oven. And because no baking is required, these recipes are perfect for you first-time bakers out there! For most of the recipes, all you need is a food processor, mixing bowl and a saucepan. All these recipes are quick, easy and foolproof!

You will absolutely want to make the Cookies and Cream Tart (page 103), Chocolate Chip Cookie Dough Pie (page 108), Strawberry Lemonade Tart (page 111) and so many more recipes! No one will even know they are vegan, let alone no-bake!

# CREAMY MASCARPONE FIG TART

Yield: 1 (9" [23-cm]) tart

This tart features not only fresh, ripe figs but also a creamy, lemony mascarpone filling and a delicious two-ingredient graham crust. It is deceptively easy to make and a showstopper dessert that will wow all your family and friends.

### For the Crust
1 Vegan Graham Crust (page 17)

### For the Filling
227 g (8 oz) vegan cream cheese, room temperature

80 g (⅓ cup) coconut cream

50 g (½ cup) powdered sugar

30 ml (2 tbsp) fresh lemon juice

Zest of 1 lemon

10 g (2 tsp) pure vanilla extract

½ tsp ground cinnamon

½ tsp ground ginger

⅛ tsp fine sea salt

### For the Topping
454 g (16 oz) fresh, ripe figs, sliced thinly

Make the Vegan Graham Crust and place it in the refrigerator for 1 hour while you make the filling.

To make the filling, add the vegan cream cheese to a bowl, and whip with a hand mixer until it is smooth, about 15 seconds. Add the coconut cream, powdered sugar, lemon juice, lemon zest, vanilla extract, cinnamon, ginger and salt. Mix with the hand mixer until well combined, scraping the sides as needed. Pour the filling into the tart crust. Top the crust with the sliced figs and transfer the tart to the refrigerator to set for 1 hour before serving.

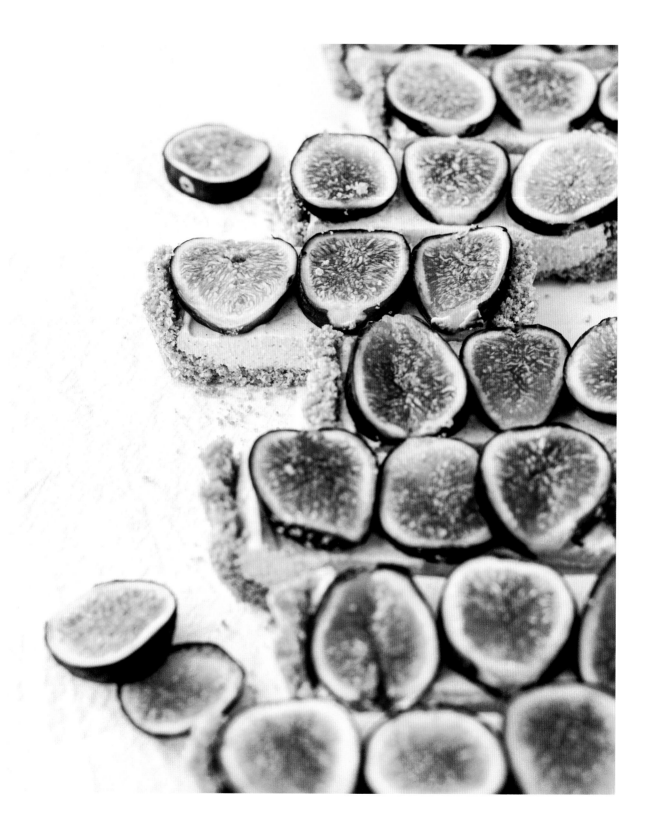

# COOKIES AND CREAM TART

## Yield: 1 (9" [23-cm]) tart

This rich and decadent tart will make you want to reach for bite after bite! It tastes just like the classic childhood favorite Oreo® cookies but made even more indulgent and irresistible. You can make it gluten-free with vegan and gluten-free chocolate cream-filled cookies.

---

### For the Crust
1 Vegan Cookies and Cream Crust (page 18)

### For the Filling
227 g (8 oz) vegan cream cheese, room temperature

240 ml (1 cup) coconut cream

50 g (¼ cup) cane sugar

1 tsp pure vanilla extract

135 g (5 oz) vegan chocolate cream-filled cookies, chopped (about 10 cookies)

### For the Topping (optional)
Chopped vegan chocolate cream-filled cookies

Make the Vegan Cookies and Cream Crust and place it in the refrigerator to chill for 1 hour while you make the filling.

To make the filling, add the vegan cream cheese to a bowl, and whip with a hand mixer until it is smooth, about 15 seconds. Add the coconut cream, sugar and vanilla extract. Mix with the hand mixer until well combined, scraping the sides as needed. Fold in the cookie pieces. Pour the filling into the crust. Place the tart in the refrigerator to set for at least 1 hour before serving, topped with additional cookies (if using).

# PUMPKIN MOUSSE TARTLETS

## Yield: 6 (3" [8-cm]) tartlets

Pumpkin pies always hold a special place in my heart, as it was the first pie I ever learned to bake. Whenever Thanksgiving or Christmas rolls around, pumpkin pie is bound to be on our menu . . . but we all know how frantic the holidays can be and how busy our ovens will be. To make it easier, these tartlets can be made a few days in advance and still taste absolutely delightful. Forget about store-bought pumpkin pie and turn to these no-bake tartlets with their creamy, silky filling and warming spices that will please all eaters!

### For the Crust
1 No-Bake Medjool Date Tart Crust (page 25)

### For the Filling
114 g (4 oz) vegan cream cheese, room temperature
120 g (½ cup) pumpkin puree
120 g (½ cup) coconut cream
65 ml (~3 tbsp) maple syrup
4 g (1¼ tsp) ground cinnamon
¾ tsp ground ginger
⅛ tsp ground nutmeg
Dash of ground cloves
Pinch of fine sea salt

Make the crust, but divide the dough among six (3-inch [8-cm]) tartlet pans, pressing on the sides until the dough covers the pans. Place the crusts in the refrigerator until the filling is ready.

To make the filling, add the vegan cream cheese to a bowl and whip with a hand mixer until it is smooth and creamy, about 15 seconds. Add the pumpkin puree, coconut cream, maple syrup, cinnamon, ginger, nutmeg, cloves and salt. Mix with the hand mixer until well combined, scraping the sides as needed.

Divide the filling among the tartlet pans and transfer them to the refrigerator to set for 2 hours before serving. Top the tarts with any leftover decorative crusts you want!

# RASPBERRY CUSTARD TARTLETS

Yield: 6 (3" [8-cm]) tartlets

I just love custards . . . all custards. When I went vegan, I worried that I couldn't have custard anymore. Silly me. Vegan custard is super easy to make. I dare say, I love it even more than the classic non-vegan custard, which is why you will fall in love with these tartlets. They are made with homemade vegan custard and topped with fresh, sweet raspberries. Best of all, their size means you won't have to worry about sharing yours with others!

### For the Crust
1 No-Bake Medjool Date Tart Crust (page 25)

### For the Filling
125 ml (½ cup) full-fat coconut milk

63 ml (¼ cup) vegan evaporated milk

67 g (⅓ cup) cane sugar

13 g (1 tbsp) vegan custard powder

½ tsp pure vanilla extract

15 g (1½ tbsp) cornstarch + 30 ml (2 tbsp) cold water, combined

### For the Topping
150 g (~1 cup + 3 tbsp) fresh raspberries

Make the crust, but divide the dough among six (3-inch [8-cm]) tartlet pans, pressing on the sides until the dough covers the pans. Place the crusts in the refrigerator until the filling is ready.

To make the filling, add the coconut milk, vegan evaporated milk, sugar, custard powder and vanilla extract to a saucepan over medium heat. Whisk all the ingredients together until there are no lumps. Once the filling starts to boil, slowly add the cornstarch slurry, stirring constantly. When the filling thickens, after 5 to 10 seconds, divide the filling among the tartlet pans, smoothing the tops. Allow the tarts to cool for 10 minutes before transferring them to the refrigerator to chill for 1 hour. Top the tartlets with the fresh raspberries before serving.

# CHOCOLATE CHIP COOKIE DOUGH PIE

## Yield: 1 (9" [23-cm]) pie

I can't get enough of the classic flavor of chocolate chip cookie dough. From ice cream to cookies to pies, you can always win me over with chocolate chip cookie dough flavor. This pie is daringly simple to make and absolutely irresistible. It features a graham crust, an oat-based cookie dough and a chocolate ganache topping with sprinkles of flaky sea salt. You won't regret making this pie!

### For the Crust

1 Vegan Graham Crust (page 17)

### For the Filling

158 g (⅔ cup + 1 tbsp) oat flour

150 g (¾ cup) cane sugar

115 g (½ cup) unsalted vegan butter, cut into 1" (2.5-cm) cubes, cold

1 tsp pure vanilla extract

⅛ tsp fine sea salt

32–48 ml (2–3 tbsp) unsweetened plant-based milk of choice

170 g (1 cup) vegan mini chocolate chips

### For the Chocolate Ganache Topping

240 ml (1 cup) coconut cream

227 g (8 oz) chopped vegan dark chocolate (or chocolate chips)

Make the Vegan Graham Crust and transfer it to the refrigerator to chill for 1 hour.

To make the filling, add the oat flour, sugar, vegan butter, vanilla extract and salt to a food processor, and blitz until all the ingredients are well combined. Add 1 tablespoon (16 ml) of the plant-based milk to the food processor at a time and pulse until a dough forms. Transfer the dough to a bowl. Fold in the vegan chocolate chips. Transfer the dough to the crust, smoothing out the top. Place the pie in the refrigerator to chill for 1 hour.

To make the chocolate ganache topping, add the coconut cream to a small saucepan and bring it to a simmer over medium heat. Place the chocolate in a heat-safe bowl, pour the coconut cream over the chocolate and let it sit for 2 to 3 minutes. Then, mix the ingredients together until it is smooth and creamy. Pour some of the chocolate ganache (you will have some leftovers) on top of the tart, spreading it evenly. Transfer the pie to the refrigerator and allow the ganache to set for 1 hour before serving.

# STRAWBERRY LEMONADE TART

## Yield: 1 (9" [23-cm]) tart

Made with fresh, seasonal strawberries and the taste of fresh lemonade, this tart is a delight during those hot, summer days. The filling is so deliciously creamy and refreshing you won't be able to resist going back for another bite!

### For the Crust
1 No-Bake Medjool Date Tart Crust (page 25)

### For the Filling
480 g (4 cups) fresh strawberries

1 (400-g [1⅔ cups]) can full-fat coconut milk

25 g (2 tbsp) cane sugar

60 ml (¼ cup) fresh lemon juice

Zest of 1 lemon

1 tsp pure vanilla extract

35 g (3½ tbsp) cornstarch + 60 ml (4 tbsp) cold water, combined

### For the Topping
60 g (½ cup) fresh strawberries, sliced

Sliced lemons (optional)

Fresh mint leaves (optional)

Chopped nuts of choice (optional)

Make the No-Bake Medjool Date Tart Crust and place it in the refrigerator until the filling is ready.

To make the filling, add the strawberries to a food processor and blend until all the berries have broken apart and the juices have been released. Pour the strawberry juice through a strainer over a bowl to remove any remaining seeds.

Add the strawberry juice, coconut milk, sugar, lemon juice, lemon zest and vanilla extract to a saucepan over medium heat. Mix all the ingredients together until they are well combined. Once the filling starts to boil, slowly add the cornstarch slurry, stirring constantly. When the filling thickens, pour it into the crust. Allow the tart to cool for 15 minutes before transferring it to the refrigerator to chill for 2 hours or overnight. Top the tart with the sliced strawberries and lemons, fresh mint and chopped nuts, if using, before serving.

# CHOCOLATE BERRY TART WITH CHOCOLATE WALNUT CRUST

## Yield: 1 (9" [23-cm]) tart

### For the Crust

200 g (1 cup) Medjool dates, soaked overnight in water, drained

150 g (1 cup + 3 tbsp) raw walnuts

33 g (⅓ cup) cacao powder

30 ml (1 tbsp + 1 tsp) maple syrup

½ tsp ground cinnamon

¼ tsp fine sea salt

### For the Berry Filling

125 g (1 cup) fresh raspberries

120 g (1 cup) fresh blackberries

150 g (1 cup) fresh blueberries

120 g (½ cup) water

43 ml (2 tbsp) maple syrup

1 tsp chia seeds

### For the Chocolate Ganache

240 ml (1 cup) coconut cream

227 g (8 oz) chopped vegan dark chocolate (or chocolate chips)

### For the Topping (optional)

75 g (½ cup) fresh mixed berries of choice

This chapter wouldn't be complete without a combination of my favorite fruits and the love of my life, chocolate. The filling in this tart is rich and creamy with sweetness from the fresh berries, which is enhanced by a chocolate walnut crust. After one bite, you will be surprised to know that it is vegan, gluten-free, refined sugar-free and oil-free!

To make the crust, add the drained dates, walnuts, cacao powder, maple syrup, cinnamon and salt to a food processor, and blend until all the ingredients come together. The dough will be slightly sticky. Transfer the dough to a 9-inch (23-cm) tart pan, pressing on the sides and bottom of the tart pan. Place the finished tart crust in the refrigerator to chill for 30 minutes.

To make the berry filling, add the raspberries, blackberries, blueberries and water to a saucepan, and bring to a simmer over medium-low heat. Break the berries into pieces with a fork. Add the maple syrup and chia seeds and stir to combine. Allow the berries to simmer for 2 to 3 minutes, or until the mixture starts to thicken slightly. Pour the berry filling into the tart crust and place it in the refrigerator to set for 1 hour.

To make the chocolate ganache, add the coconut cream to a small saucepan and bring it to a simmer over medium heat. Place the chocolate in a heat-safe bowl, pour the coconut cream over the chocolate and let it sit for 2 to 3 minutes. Mix the ingredients together until smooth and creamy.

Pour the ganache on the top of the tart, spreading it evenly. Transfer the tart to the refrigerator to set for 1 hour. Top with fresh mixed berries (if using) before serving.

# VEGAN CARROT CAKE TART

## Yield: 1 (9" [23-cm]) tart

### For the Crust

110 g (~1¼ cups) oat flour

90 g (1 cup) grated carrots

150 g (¾ cup) Medjool dates

30 g (¼ cup + 2 tbsp) shredded unsweetened coconut

23 g (3 tbsp) raw walnuts

¾ tsp ground cinnamon

½ tsp ground ginger

⅛ tsp ground allspice

⅛ tsp fine sea salt

### For the Filling

98 g (¾ cup) raw cashews, soaked overnight in water

85 g (3 oz) vegan cream cheese, room temperature

120 ml (½ cup) coconut cream

113 ml (⅓ cup) maple syrup

30 g (2 tbsp) unrefined coconut oil, melted

½ tsp ground cinnamon

¼ tsp ground nutmeg

### For the Topping (optional)

48 g (½ cup) vegan whipped cream

Natural green and orange vegan food coloring

Shredded coconut

I didn't discover carrot cake until much later in life when I was in college. Since then, carrot cake has become one of my favorite desserts. This tart is healthy and made entirely in a food processor! The carrot cake crust is naturally sweetened and packed with delicious textures and topped with a creamy coconut cream cheese filling with warming spices from the cinnamon and nutmeg.

To make the crust, add the oat flour, carrots, dates, shredded coconut, walnuts, cinnamon, ginger, allspice and salt to a food processor, and blend until all the ingredients come together into a dough. Transfer the dough to a 9-inch (23-cm) tart pan, pressing on the sides and bottom. Place the finished tart crust in the refrigerator to chill for 30 minutes.

To make the filling, add the cashews, vegan cream cheese, coconut cream, maple syrup, coconut oil, cinnamon and nutmeg to a food processor, and blend until well combined and smooth. Pour the filling into the crust and transfer it to the refrigerator to chill for 2 hours.

To make the topping (if using), divide the vegan whipped cream into two bowls. Add a very small drop of green food coloring to one bowl and orange food coloring to the other. Mix until the colors are incorporated. Transfer the whipped toppings to two piping bags. To make the carrot shapes, use the orange topping to pipe a small triangle to the top of the filling. Make leaf shapes using the green topping. Repeat the steps and decorate the tart however you like, finishing with shredded coconut, if using.

# BLUEBERRY LEMON CURD TART

Yield: 1 (9" [23-cm]) pie

I fell in love with lemon curd while studying abroad in Paris, which is heaven for foodies. It was during one of our class outings that my professor introduced us to the best lemon curd tart I've ever tasted. It was refreshing, tangy and sweetened just enough so it didn't overpower the citrus flavors. Since then, I have been on the hunt for the best vegan lemon curd tart, which led me to this recipe. One bite will transport me back to Paris, enjoying that lemon curd tart. This lemon curd is vegan with coconut cream and fresh lemon juice.

### For the Crust
1 No-Bake Medjool Date Tart Crust (page 25)

### For the Lemon Curd Filling
240 ml (1 cup) coconut cream

240 ml (1 cup) fresh lemon juice

Zest of 1 lemon

200 g (1 cup) cane sugar

⅛ tsp fine sea salt

Dash of ground turmeric (optional for color)

30 g (3 tbsp) cornstarch + 30 ml (2 tbsp) cold water, combined

### For the Topping
75 g (½ cup) fresh blueberries

Sliced lemons (optional)

Mint leaves (optional)

Make the No-Bake Medjool Date Tart Crust and place it in the refrigerator until the filling is ready.

To make the lemon curd filling, add the coconut cream, lemon juice, lemon zest, sugar, salt and ground turmeric (if using) to a saucepan over medium heat. Stir until well combined. Once the filling starts to boil, slowly add the cornstarch slurry, stirring constantly. When the filling starts to thicken, about 30 seconds, pour the lemon curd into the crust. Allow the tart to cool for 15 minutes before transferring it to the refrigerator to chill for 2 hours or overnight. Top the tarts with the fresh blueberries, sliced lemon and mint leaves (if using) when ready to serve.

# INDULGENT CHOCOLATE GANACHE TART

**Yield: 1 (9" [23-cm]) pie**

**For the Crust**
1 Vegan Cookies and Cream Crust (page 18)

**For the Chocolate Ganache Filling**
360 g (1½ cups) coconut cream
60 g (¼ cup) unsalted vegan butter
283 g (10 oz) chopped vegan dark chocolate (or chocolate chips)

**For the Topping**
1 tsp fine sea salt flakes

The richer and darker the chocolate, the more I will love the dessert. This is just my personal preference, of course, and you can use any chopped vegan dark chocolate you want in this recipe. This deceptively simple tart features the no-bake Vegan Cookies and Cream Crust (page 18) that requires no dough-making skills and can be made gluten-free, as well as an indulgent, creamy dark chocolate filling topped with flaky sea salt. This luxurious tart is most certainly a showstopper.

Make the Vegan Cookies and Cream Crust and transfer it to the refrigerator to chill for 1 hour.

To make the filling, add the coconut cream and vegan butter to a saucepan, and bring it to a simmer over medium heat. Place the chocolate in a heat-safe bowl, pour the coconut cream over the chocolate and let it sit for 2 to 3 minutes. Mix the ingredients together with a spatula until smooth and creamy. Pour the filling into the crust, spreading it evenly. Transfer the tart to the refrigerator and let it set for 1 hour. Sprinkle salt flakes over the pie when ready to serve.

# CHOCOLATE AVOCADO MOUSSE TART

Yield: 1 9" (23-cm) tart

This decadent and creamy tart is enveloped by the Vegan Cookies and Cream Crust (page 18) and is silky smooth and oh, so delicious. It is secretly healthy with ripe avocados and maple syrup. This is one of those recipes that my friends are always asking me to make over and over again!

### For the Crust
1 Vegan Cookies and Cream Crust (page 18)

### For the Filling
170 g (6 oz) chopped vegan dark chocolate (or chocolate chips)

30 g (2 tbsp) unrefined coconut oil

300 g (2 large) pitted ripe avocados

170 ml (½ cup) maple syrup

1 tsp pure vanilla extract

¼ tsp fine sea salt

### For the Topping
150 g (1 cup) fresh mixed berries

Make the Vegan Cookies and Cream Crust and transfer it to the refrigerator to chill for 1 hour.

To make the filling, add the chocolate and coconut oil to a glass bowl. Microwave it in 15-second intervals until all the chocolate has melted. Add the melted chocolate, avocados, maple syrup, vanilla extract and salt to a food processor, and blend until smooth and creamy, scraping down the sides as needed. Transfer the filling to the prepared crust, smoothing out the top. Place the tart in the refrigerator to set for 1 hour. Top the tart with fresh berries when ready to serve.

# SWEET AND SAVORY GALETTES

During the summer before my junior year in college, I was given the opportunity to study abroad in Paris to take a creative food writing course. Yes, a class all on food in the City of Love! My English professor had previously lived as a chef in Paris. She returned almost every year, taking a new group of students to learn about the food culture there.

Prior to our trip, my professor arranged a dinner for our small class at her home. There was only a handful of us, but I remember that when we arrived I felt like I had just walked into an old French country kitchen. The kitchen island was made of rustic wood with a chopping board top. The walls were lined with spices from all around the world. She had a small antique stovetop with an antique bread oven (picture the wood-fired ones but about the size of a box). I felt like I had stepped into another world.

When we were done with dinner, my professor pulled a strawberry rhubarb galette out of the oven. I watched in fascination at the amount of care she put into slicing the galette and serving it with a scoop of ice cream. It was the first time I had rhubarb and also a galette, and that's when I fell in love with them both. I loved the tartness of the rhubarb combined with the sweetness from the strawberries and the buttery crust. Just sitting in her kitchen I felt like I was already in Paris.

Every time I think about galettes, I return to that memory. So, when I sat down to write this book, I knew without a doubt that there would be a galette chapter. Here you will find both sweet and savory galette recipes, perfect for when you want to make a quick dinner or dessert. You don't want to miss out on the Caramelized Onion, Corn and Tomato Galette (page 140), made with juicy summer tomatoes and corn, the Rustic Summer Peach Galette (page 132) or the Mini Blueberry Lavender Galettes (page 128). Don't forget to top the sweet ones with a scoop of ice cream!

# RASPBERRY GINGER STONE FRUIT GALETTE

## Yield: 1 galette

I just love stone fruits so much . . . all of them. They're sweet and juicy when ripe and are the perfect summer snacks. It would not be summer without a stone fruit galette. Between the buttery dough and the sweet, juicy filling, there is really no reason at all not to make it!

### For the Crust
1 Buttery Vegan Galette Crust (page 14)

### For the Filling
520 g (4 cups) ripe stone fruits of choice, sliced thinly

125 g (1 cup) fresh raspberries

80 g (½ cup) coconut sugar

15 g (1" [2.5-cm]) piece fresh ginger, grated

8 ml (½ tbsp) fresh lemon juice

Zest of 1 lemon

10 g (1 tbsp) cornstarch

### For the Glaze
10 ml (½ tbsp) maple syrup

28 g (2 tbsp) unsalted vegan butter, melted

Coarse sugar, for sprinkling

### For the Topping (optional)
Vegan vanilla ice cream

Preheat the oven to 375°F (190°C).

Make the Buttery Vegan Galette Crust and allow the dough to chill in the refrigerator while you prepare the filling.

To make the filling, add the stone fruits, raspberries, sugar, ginger, lemon juice, lemon zest and cornstarch to a bowl and toss. Let the filling sit for 20 minutes to allow the juices to come out.

To make the glaze, add the maple syrup and vegan butter to a small bowl, and mix well. Set aside.

Take the dough out of the refrigerator and place it between two pieces of parchment paper. Roll the dough into a circle that's 12 inches (30 cm) in diameter. Slide the rolled dough onto a baking sheet.

Using a slotted spoon, spread the filling, without the juices, on the dough, leaving 2 inches (5 cm) around the edge bare. Fold the edges of the dough up over the filling to form the crust. Place the galette in the freezer for 5 minutes. Remove the galette from the freezer and brush the crust with the glaze and sprinkle some coarse sugar around the crust. Bake for 25 to 30 minutes, or until the crust turns lightly golden brown. Top the galette with a scoop of vegan vanilla ice cream, if using, before serving.

# SUMMER MIXED BERRY GALETTE

### Yield: 1 galette

Nothing highlights summer more than this mixed berry galette. It is truly foolproof to assemble, making it perfect for anyone making a galette for the first time! Feel free to substitute any other berries you desire, and don't forget a scoop of ice cream!

### For the Crust
1 Buttery Vegan Galette Crust (page 14)

### For the Filling
150 g (1 cup) fresh blueberries

125 g (1 cup) fresh raspberries

120 g (1 cup) fresh strawberries, sliced thinly

100 g (½ cup) cane sugar

15 ml (1 tbsp) fresh lemon juice

Zest of 1 lemon

20 g (2 tbsp) arrowroot powder

### For the Glaze
10 ml (½ tbsp) maple syrup

28 g (2 tbsp) unsalted vegan butter, melted

Coarse sugar, for sprinkling

Preheat the oven to 400°F (205°C).

Make the Vegan Galette Crust and allow the dough to chill in the refrigerator while you prepare the filling.

To make the filling, add the blueberries, raspberries, strawberries, sugar, lemon juice, lemon zest and arrowroot powder to a bowl and toss. Let the filling sit for 10 minutes.

To make the glaze, add the maple syrup and vegan butter to a small bowl, and mix well. Set aside.

Take the dough out of the refrigerator and place it between two pieces of parchment paper. Roll the dough into a circle that's 12 inches (30 cm) in diameter. Slide the rolled dough onto a baking sheet.

Spread the filling on the dough, leaving 2 inches (5 cm) around the edge bare. Fold the edges of the dough up over the filling to form the crust. Place the galette in the freezer for 5 minutes. Remove the galette from the freezer, brush the crust with the glaze and sprinkle coarse sugar around the crust. Bake for 25 to 30 minutes, or until the berries are juicy and the crust turns lightly golden brown.

# MINI BLUEBERRY LAVENDER GALETTES

## Yield: 6 mini galettes

### For the Crust
1 Buttery Vegan Galette Crust (page 14)

### For the Filling
450 g (3 cups) fresh blueberries

100 g (½ cup) cane sugar

15 ml (1 tbsp) lemon juice

Zest of 1 lemon

1 tsp pure vanilla extract

3 g (1 tbsp) food-grade lavender flowers

20 g (2 tbsp) arrowroot powder

### For the Glaze
10 ml (½ tbsp) maple syrup

28 g (2 tbsp) unsalted vegan butter, melted

Coarse sugar, for sprinkling

Ever since I was little, I've been obsessed with blueberries. I love their cute size and the beautiful hue of blue and purple that they have. Whenever blueberries were on sale, especially during the summer months, my mom would buy me cases and cases of them, and I would finish them all in less than a week. I can still do the same, but after learning to make galettes, making a blueberry galette during the summer with fresh blueberries is a must-do for me. One of the best flavors (in my opinion) to pair with blueberries is lavender, which is another reason why I am obsessed with these mini galettes. Words cannot possibly express how delicious they are. Juicy, sweet blueberries meet a flaky crust with hints of lavender . . . it will leave you wanting more.

---

Preheat the oven to 400°F (205°C).

Make the Buttery Vegan Galette Crust and allow the dough to chill in the refrigerator while you prepare the filling.

To make the filling, add the blueberries, sugar, lemon juice, lemon zest, vanilla extract, lavender flowers and arrowroot powder to a bowl and toss. Let the filling sit for 15 minutes.

To make the glaze, add the maple syrup and vegan butter to a small bowl, and mix well. Set aside.

Take the dough out of the refrigerator and divide it into six equal portions. Place one of the pieces of dough between two pieces of parchment paper. Roll the dough into a circle that's 6 inches (15 cm) in diameter. Slide the rolled dough onto a baking sheet.

Spread the blueberry filling over the dough, leaving 1 inch (2.5 cm) around the edge bare. Fold the edges of the dough up over the filling to form the crust. Repeat with the remaining dough. Place the galettes in the freezer for 5 minutes. Remove the galettes from the freezer, brush the crusts with the glaze and sprinkle coarse sugar around the crusts. Bake for 25 to 30 minutes, or until the crusts turn lightly golden brown and the blueberries are bursting with their juices.

# ROASTED GRAPE GALETTE WITH ALMOND CREAM

## Yield: 1 galette

### For the Crust
1 Buttery Vegan Galette Crust (page 14)

### For the Almond Cream
80 g (½ cup) blanched almonds, soaked overnight

32 ml (2 tbsp) unsweetened plant-based milk of choice

15 g (1 tbsp) unrefined coconut oil, melted

15 ml (1 tbsp) fresh lemon juice

⅛ tsp fine sea salt

### For the Filling
400 g (2 cups) seedless grapes (if the grapes are large, slice them in half)

80 g (½ cup) coconut sugar

Zest of 1 lemon

10 g (1 tbsp) cornstarch

### For the Glaze
10 ml (½ tbsp) maple syrup

28 g (2 tbsp) unsalted vegan butter, melted

### For the Topping
Sliced almonds

Coarse sugar

In my mom's garden, she has a little corner dedicated to a grapevine. Every summer, when the grapes become ripe, bees would swarm that area. My parents and I would wear long sleeves and pants and large hats to cover our bodies. We'd go in quickly to pick out bunches and bunches of ripe grapes while avoiding the bees. When we were done, and if it was a good harvest, we would have buckets of grapes lining the outside of our house, waiting for us to eat. So, what better time than right then to make a grape galette? With simple ingredients, a natural sweetness, a crumbly flaky crust and homemade vegan almond cheese, this galette has all the homey and cozy goodness you're craving!

---

Preheat the oven to 375°F (190°C).

Make the Buttery Vegan Galette Crust and allow the dough to chill in the refrigerator while you prepare the filling.

To make the almond cream, add the almonds, plant-based milk, coconut oil, lemon juice and salt to a food processor. Blend until smooth and creamy. Transfer to a bowl and place it in the refrigerator to chill for 30 minutes.

To make the filling, add the grapes, sugar, lemon zest and cornstarch to a bowl and toss. Allow the filling to sit for 10 minutes.

To make the glaze, add the maple syrup and vegan butter to a small bowl, and mix well.

Take the dough out of the refrigerator and place it between two pieces of parchment paper. Roll the dough into a circle that's 12 inches (30 cm) in diameter. Slide the rolled dough onto a baking sheet.

Spread the almond cream on the dough, leaving 2 inches (5 cm) around the edge bare. Top the almond cream with the grape filling. Fold the edges of the dough up over the filling to form the crust. Place the galette in the freezer for 5 minutes. Remove the galette from the freezer, brush the crust with the glaze and sprinkle sliced almonds and coarse sugar around the crust. Bake for 40 to 45 minutes, or until the grapes are tender and the crust turns lightly golden brown.

# RUSTIC SUMMER PEACH GALETTE

### Yield: 1 galette

Juicy, ripe summer peaches meet a flaky buttery crust that will leave you wanting to reach in for another slice right away! Nothing captures the epitome of summer quite like this galette. Top it with a scoop of vegan vanilla ice cream, and it deserves a chef's kiss!

### For the Crust
1 Buttery Vegan Galette Crust (page 14)

### For the Filling
573 g (5 large) ripe peaches, peeled and sliced thinly
50 g (¼ cup) cane sugar
15 ml (1 tbsp) fresh lemon juice
Zest of 1 lemon
4 g (1½ tsp) arrowroot powder

### For the Glaze
10 ml (½ tbsp) maple syrup
28 g (2 tbsp) unsalted vegan butter, melted
Coarse sugar, for sprinkling

### For the Topping (optional)
Fresh thyme leaves

Preheat the oven to 400°F (205°C).

Make the Buttery Vegan Galette Crust and let it chill in the refrigerator while you prepare the filling.

To make the filling, add the peaches, sugar, lemon juice, lemon zest and arrowroot powder to a bowl and toss. Let the filling sit for 20 minutes or until the juices release.

To make the glaze, add the maple syrup and vegan butter to a small bowl, and mix well.

Take the dough out of the refrigerator and place it between two pieces of parchment paper. Roll the dough into a circle that's 12 inches (30 cm) in diameter. Slide the rolled dough onto a baking sheet.

Spread the filling without the juices over the dough, leaving about 2 inches (5 cm) around the edge bare. Fold the edges of the dough up over the filling to form the crust. Place the galette in the freezer for 5 minutes. Remove the galette from the freezer, brush it with the glaze and sprinkle coarse sugar around the crust. Bake for 40 to 45 minutes, or until the crust turns lightly golden brown. Top the galette with some fresh thyme leaves, if using, before serving.

# SPICED PEAR AND WALNUT GALETTE

## Yield: 1 galette

### For the Crust
1 Buttery Vegan Galette Crust
(page 14)

### For the Filling
750 g (4 large) ripe pears of choice,
peeled, cored and sliced into
½" (1-cm)-thick wedges

50 g (¼ cup) cane sugar

28 g (2 tbsp) unsalted vegan butter,
melted

8 g (1 tbsp) all-purpose flour

1 tsp ground cinnamon

1 tsp ground coriander

½ tsp ground ginger

½ tsp ground nutmeg

40 g (⅓ cup) walnuts, chopped

### For the Glaze
10 ml (½ tbsp) maple syrup

28 g (2 tbsp) unsalted vegan butter,
melted

Coarse sugar, for sprinkling

### For the Topping (optional)
Vegan vanilla ice cream

The pear tree in my mother's garden produced plenty of pears, so I would try to bake with them as often as I could so they did not turn bad. Pear pies were what I made most of the time, knowing my mom liked pies more than cakes or bread. It is something she doesn't have often, and to this day it is one of the few American desserts she likes. When my pie was done, the smell of the buttery crust and the sweetness of the pears would fill the house. Everyone would come downstairs wondering what I made. As soon as the pie cooled, I would cut a slice for my mom, so she could have the first piece. I loved the joy on her face when she took the first bite, surprised that I could actually make a pie by myself.

Trust me, I am surprised as well, whenever I play in the kitchen, trying new recipes. This experimentation led to this galette. It has everything I crave during the fall: warm spices, juicy pears enveloped in a buttery crust and an extra touch of crunch from the walnuts. One bite instantly sends me back to my childhood in my mom's kitchen.

---

Preheat the oven to 375°F (190°C).

Make the Buttery Vegan Galette Crust and let it chill in the refrigerator while you prepare the filling.

To make the filling, add the pears, sugar, vegan butter, flour, cinnamon, coriander, ginger and nutmeg to a bowl and toss. Let the filling sit for 20 minutes, or until the juices release.

To make the glaze, add the maple syrup and vegan butter to a small bowl, and mix well.

Take the dough out of the refrigerator and place it between two pieces of parchment paper. Roll the dough into a circle that's 12 inches (30 cm) in diameter. Slide the rolled dough onto a baking sheet.

Using a slotted spoon, spread the filling without the juices over the dough, leaving about 2 inches (5 cm) around the edge bare. Fold the edges of the dough up over the filling to form the crust. Place the galette in the freezer for 5 minutes. Remove the galette from the freezer, brush it with the glaze and sprinkle coarse sugar around the crust. Top with the chopped walnuts. Bake for 30 to 35 minutes, or until the pears are soft and the crust turns lightly golden brown. Top the galette with some vegan vanilla ice cream, if using, before serving!

# ROASTED BEET AND SWEET POTATOES GALETTE

## Yield: 1 galette

### For the Crust
1 Buttery Vegan Galette Crust (page 14)

30 ml (2 tbsp) unsweetened plant-based milk of choice

### For the Filling
28 g (2 tbsp) unsalted vegan butter, melted

13 g (3 small) garlic cloves, minced

65 g (½ cup) sweet Vidalia onion, diced

1 tsp red wine vinegar

¼ tsp fine sea salt

½ tsp black pepper

85 g (3 oz) vegan cream cheese, room temperature

100 g (3½ oz) crumbled vegan feta, divided

1 tsp fresh thyme, chopped

### For the Topping
145 g (1 small) Japanese sweet potato, sliced ¼" (6 mm) thick

145 g (1 small) regular sweet potato, sliced ¼" (6 mm) thick

155 g (2 small) red beets

55 g (1 small) orange beets

Olive oil, for drizzling

Crumbled vegan feta cheese

Beets and sweet potatoes are my favorite root vegetables. This simple galette layers sweet root vegetables over a creamy vegan cream cheese and feta spread baked in a flaky, buttery crust. Make it for brunch or dinner and be prepared for your family to want another slice right away!

Preheat the oven to 375°F (190°C).

Make the Buttery Vegan Galette Crust and let it chill in the refrigerator while you prepare the filling.

To make the filling, add the vegan butter, garlic, onion, red wine vinegar, salt and pepper to a saucepan over medium heat. Cook, stirring constantly for 5 minutes, or until the onions begin to soften. Transfer to a bowl to cool. Add the cooled onions, vegan cream cheese, 85 grams (3 oz) of the vegan feta and thyme to the bowl with the onions, and mix until well combined. Set aside.

Take the dough out of the refrigerator and place it between two pieces of parchment paper. Roll the dough into a circle that's 12 inches (30 cm) in diameter. Slide the rolled dough onto a baking sheet.

Spread the filling on the dough, leaving 2 inches (5 cm) around the edge bare. Top the filling with the sliced sweet potatoes and beets. Fold the edges of the dough up over the filling to form the crust. Place the galette in the freezer for 5 minutes. Remove the galette from the freezer and sprinkle the remaining vegan feta cheese over the crust. Brush the crust with the plant-based milk. Bake for 40 to 45 minutes, or until the vegetables are tender and the crust turns lightly golden brown. Once it is ready, drizzle on some olive oil and top with additional vegan feta cheese.

# LEMONY RICOTTA SUMMER SQUASH GALETTE

Yield: 1 galette

Cheesy and creamy vegan lemon ricotta meets sweet summer squash wrapped in a delicious, buttery crust. This rustic tart is easy to make and tastes fabulous whether it is hot, cold or warm. It is perfect for busy weeknights and as a light meal or appetizer!

### For the Crust

1 Buttery Vegan Galette Crust (page 14)

30 ml (2 tbsp) unsweetened plant-based milk of choice

### For the Filling

250 g (1 cup) vegan ricotta

20 g (¼ cup) vegan Parmesan cheese, grated

420 g (3 cups) summer squash, sliced thinly

15 ml (1 tbsp) extra virgin olive oil

15 ml (1 tbsp) fresh lemon juice

Zest of 1 lemon

4 g (1 small) garlic clove, minced

¼ tsp fine sea salt

¼ tsp black pepper

### For the Topping

1 tsp chopped fresh thyme

Preheat the oven to 400°F (205°C).

Make the Buttery Vegan Galette Crust and let it chill in the refrigerator while you prepare the filling.

To make the filling, add the vegan ricotta and vegan Parmesan cheeses to a bowl, and combine well. Set aside. In a separate bowl, add the summer squash, olive oil, lemon juice, lemon zest, garlic, salt and pepper, and toss to combine.

Take the prepared dough out of the refrigerator. Place the dough between two pieces of parchment paper. Roll the dough into a circle that's 12 inches (30 cm) in diameter. Slide the rolled dough onto a baking sheet.

Spread the vegan ricotta cheese mixture on the dough, leaving 2 inches (5 cm) around the edge bare. Top with the summer squash filling. Fold the edges of the dough up over the filling to form the crust. Place the galette in the freezer for 5 minutes. Remove the galette from the freezer, brush the crust with the plant-based milk and bake for 35 to 40 minutes, or until the squash is tender and the crust turns lightly golden brown. Top with the chopped thyme when ready to serve.

# CARAMELIZED ONION, CORN AND TOMATO GALETTE

### Yield: 1 galette

Get ready for the BEST tomato galette you will ever try! Fresh, seasonal corn and juicy tomatoes pair perfectly with caramelized onions, cheesy vegan ricotta and a flaky, buttery crust. It is an easy, yet impressive recipe that will delight the taste buds of all family and friends.

### For the Crust

1 Buttery Vegan Galette Crust (page 14)

30 ml (2 tbsp) unsweetened plant-based milk of choice

### For the Filling

45 g (3 tbsp) unsalted vegan butter

20 g (1 small head) fresh garlic, minced

150 g (~1 small) sweet Vidalia onion, sliced thinly

¼ tsp fine sea salt

¼ tsp black pepper

¼ tsp brown sugar

160 g (1¼ cups) fresh sweet corn

200 g (1 cup) vegan ricotta, room temperature

300 g (2 cups) cherry tomatoes, halved

8 ml (½ tbsp) extra virgin olive oil

3 thyme sprigs

9 g (4 tbsp) fresh basil, chopped

Preheat the oven to 400°F (205°C).

Make the Buttery Vegan Galette Crust and let it chill in the refrigerator while you prepare the filling.

To make the filling, add the vegan butter to a saucepan over medium heat. Add the garlic, onion, salt and pepper. Cook, stirring constantly for 3 to 4 minutes, or until the onion begins to soften. Add the brown sugar, stir and cook for another 2 to 3 minutes, or until the onion turns golden brown. Add the corn and cook until the corn turns lightly golden brown. Transfer the filling to a bowl and let it cool.

Take the prepared dough out of the refrigerator. Place the dough between two pieces of parchment paper. Roll the dough into a circle that's 12 inches (30 cm) in diameter. Slide the rolled dough onto a baking sheet.

Spread the vegan ricotta over the dough, leaving about 2 inches (5 cm) at the edge bare. Spread the corn and onion filling on top of the vegan ricotta. Layer the tomatoes over the caramelized corn and onion filling. Drizzle the olive oil over the tomatoes. Sprinkle on the thyme and basil. Fold the edges of the dough up over the filling to form the crust. Place the galette in the freezer for 5 minutes. Remove the galette from the freezer and brush the crust with the plant-based milk. Bake for 40 to 45 minutes, or until the crust turns lightly golden brown.

# BUTTERNUT SQUASH AND BRUSSELS SPROUTS GALETTE

Yield: 1 galette

Buttery Parmesan-covered butternut squash and Brussels sprouts join together to make an elegant, rustic tart. The sweetness from the squash pairs well with the saltiness of the Parmesan, and along with the fresh herbs, it's perfect for any novice cook and works well as a fall or winter meal or party appetizer!

### For the Crust
1 Buttery Vegan Galette Crust (page 14)

30 ml (2 tbsp) unsweetened plant-based milk of choice

### For the Filling
450 g (~3 cups) butternut squash, cut into ¼" (6-mm) cubes

125 g (1 cup) shaved Brussels sprouts

15 ml (1 tbsp) extra virgin olive oil

½ tsp fine sea salt

½ tsp black pepper

16 g (4 small) garlic cloves, minced

15 ml (1 tbsp) fresh lemon juice

5 g (2 tbsp) fresh herbs of choice (I used rosemary and thyme)

40 g (½ cup) vegan Parmesan, grated

14 g (1 tbsp) unsalted vegan butter, cut into ¼" (6-mm) cubes, cold

### For the Topping
Grated vegan Parmesan

Preheat the oven to 400°F (205°C). Line a baking sheet with parchment paper.

Make the Buttery Vegan Galette Crust and let it chill in the refrigerator while you prepare the filling.

To make the filling, add the butternut squash, Brussels sprouts, olive oil, salt and pepper to a bowl and toss. Transfer to the prepared baking sheet and bake for 20 minutes. Remove from the oven and allow the mixture to cool for 20 minutes. Do not turn off the oven.

Add the squash and Brussels sprouts mixture, garlic, lemon juice, herbs and vegan Parmesan to a bowl and toss. Set aside.

Take the prepared dough out of the refrigerator. Place the dough between two pieces of parchment paper. Roll the dough into a circle that's 12 inches (30 cm) in diameter. Slide the rolled dough onto a baking sheet.

Spread the filling on the dough, leaving 2 inches (5 cm) around the edge bare. Sprinkle the vegan butter over the galette. Fold the edges of the dough up over the filling to form the crust. Place the galette in the freezer for 5 minutes. Remove the galette from the freezer and brush the crust with the plant-based milk. Bake for 35 to 40 minutes, or until the crust turns lightly golden brown. Top with vegan Parmesan before serving.

# SAVORY SWISS CHARD AND MUSHROOM GALETTE

### Yield: 1 galette

### For the Crust

1 Buttery Vegan Galette Crust (page 14)

30 ml (2 tbsp) unsweetened plant-based milk of choice

### For the Filling

30 ml (2 tbsp) extra virgin olive oil

13 g (3 small) garlic cloves, minced

150 g (1 small) sweet Vidalia onion, sliced thinly

¼ tsp fine sea salt

¼ tsp black pepper

226 g (8 oz) cremini mushrooms, sliced

60 g (1 cup packed) Swiss chard, chopped into bite-sized pieces

1 tsp balsamic vinegar

200 g (1 cup) vegan ricotta

### For the Topping

30 g (¾ cup) fresh herbs of choice, minced

I know some people don't care for mushrooms, but I am an absolute lover of mushrooms . . . all kinds of mushrooms. There are so many varieties, and they all have a unique taste, which is one of the reasons why I love this galette so much. Rustic and flavorful, this vegan mushroom galette is filled with creamy vegan ricotta and topped with fresh Swiss chard and a variety of herbs. It is the perfect tart for entertaining!

Preheat the oven to 400°F (205°C).

Make the Buttery Vegan Galette Crust and let it chill in the refrigerator while you prepare the filling.

To make the filling, add the olive oil to a saucepan over medium heat. Once hot, add the garlic, onion, salt and pepper. Cook, stirring constantly for 5 minutes, or until the onion begins to soften. Add the mushrooms and cook for 5 to 8 minutes, or until the mushrooms are cooked. Transfer to a bowl and let the mixture cool. In a separate bowl, add the Swiss chard and balsamic vinegar, and toss to combine. Set aside.

Take the prepared dough out of the refrigerator. Place the dough between two pieces of parchment paper. Roll the dough into a circle that's 12 inches (30 cm) in diameter. Slide the rolled dough onto a baking sheet.

Spread the vegan ricotta over the dough, leaving about 2 inches (5 cm) around the edge bare. Top the vegan ricotta with the mushroom filling followed by the Swiss chard. Fold the edges of the dough up over the filling to form the crust. Place the galette in the freezer for 5 minutes. Remove the galette from the freezer and brush the crust with the plant-based milk. Bake for 35 to 40 minutes, or until the crust turns lightly golden brown. Top with the fresh herbs when ready to serve.

# ACKNOWLEDGMENTS

To my community at With Helen (formerly A StepFull of You), I am incredibly grateful for each and every one of you. Thank you to everyone who has taken the time to make one of my recipes and message me about how much you and your family enjoyed them. Thank you for trusting me in guiding you toward some vegan (and sometimes gluten-free!) sweetness in your life. Thank you, also, for supporting me these last couple of years as I delved into this world of creating fun and easy recipes. Some days can be difficult, and there are times when I want to just give up and walk away from everything, but your kindness and encouragement allowed me to continue. No words can describe how grateful I am for all of you. Thank you for following me on this journey and watching me step into more of me.

Teresa Kim, I am beyond grateful for you and our friendship. Thank you for supporting all my wild and crazy dreams and adventures and never questioning the path I chose to take; a complete 180-degree-turn from nursing. I treasure all our FaceTime dates, even when you practically lived a day ahead of me when you were in South Korea and we tried to find a time that worked for both time zones, whether it be early morning or late at night. I am so grateful KILN brought us together. You are such a light in my life.

Melanie Torres of Headstands and Heels, thank you for being such a loving and supportive friend. Your friendship means the world to me. Thank you for making me feel welcomed and seen and for supporting my dreams. Thank you for being a cheerleader of my life and showering me with all your positive energy.

Jordan Drankoski of Dancing for Donuts, you truly are a light in this world. I still remember our first call together when I basically had zero followers on Instagram, and you trusted me to do an interview together. Thank you for being the first friend I made on social media and for supporting me these past couple of years. You inspire me every day with your loving and kind heart, passion, creativity and love for life. You remind me to enjoy every day to its fullest and that my dreams can come true.

Joanie Simon, you need an award for being the best food photographer and educator. I am extremely grateful for the knowledge you imparted to me about food photography. I wouldn't be here today without you, and with every course, video and book you create, I learn something new. You helped me think of photography in different ways, and most importantly, you remind me to have fun with it all and to enjoy the process as I continue to develop my photography skills. I am just so grateful for you. This cookbook wouldn't be possible without you.

Madeline, my editor at Page Street Publishing, thank you for helping me put this cookbook together. Thank you for being a cheerleader in making this cookbook come true. Thank you for answering the slew of emails I sent and for your kindness and patience.

The entire Page Street Publishing team, you are all incredible people. I am beyond grateful for you all and for this opportunity to work alongside you.

Lastly, to my parents. We didn't always have the best relationship, but thank you for supporting me through it all, even when you had absolutely no idea of what I was doing sometimes. You taught me at a young age to work hard, but you never pushed me to become something I did not want to be. Thank you for showering me with all your love and for trusting me through all your worries.

# ABOUT THE AUTHOR

Helen Au is the food photographer, recipe developer and content creator behind the vegan food blog, With Helen (formerly A StepFull of You). Helen comes from a long line of restaurateurs; two of her grandparents had restaurants when they lived in Vietnam. Although the restaurants no longer exist, her parents, especially her mom, passed down their love of cooking and baking to her.

After leaving nursing, Helen founded her blog with a desire to share fun, vegan recipes that everyone could enjoy with people they love. With Helen contains a variety of comforting baked goods and treats with a fun twist that makes baking a joyful process. Some of Helen's recipes are influenced by her culture, and all are made with simple plant-based ingredients and love.

When she is not in the kitchen, Helen enjoys traveling and learning about different cultures; exploring new cafes and restaurants; reading; meditating; and connecting with her friends, family and community. Most importantly, Helen believes in living life with beauty, ease, grace, adventure and lots of laughter.

# INDEX